OVER
EUROPE

GEORG GERSTER

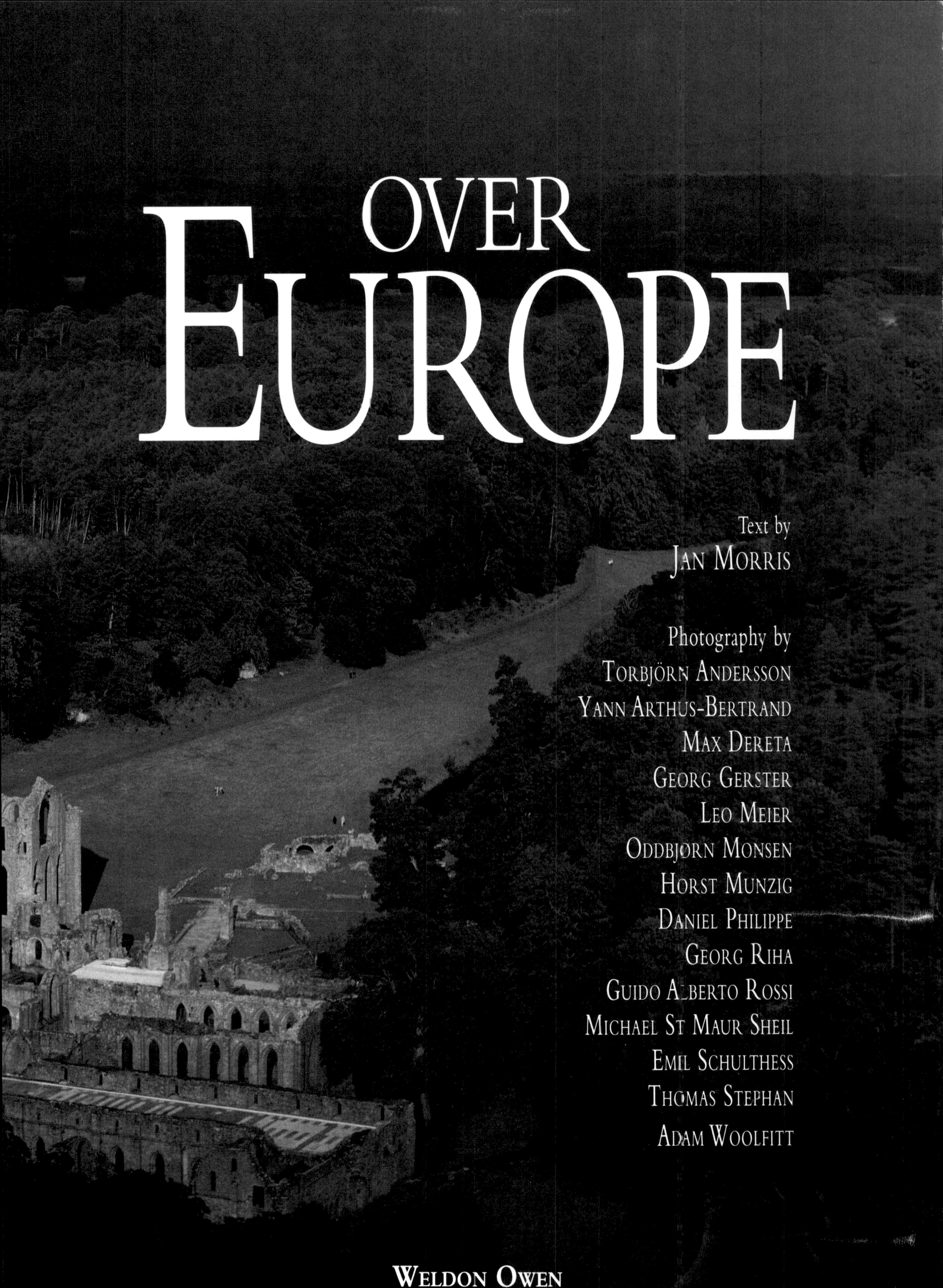

OVER
EUROPE

Text by
JAN MORRIS

Photography by
TORBJÖRN ANDERSSON
YANN ARTHUS-BERTRAND
MAX DERETA
GEORG GERSTER
LEO MEIER
ODDBJØRN MONSEN
HORST MUNZIG
DANIEL PHILIPPE
GEORG RIHA
GUIDO ALBERTO ROSSI
MICHAEL ST MAUR SHEIL
EMIL SCHULTHESS
THOMAS STEPHAN
ADAM WOOLFITT

WELDON OWEN

Over Europe
Project Team

Publisher
Robert Cave-Rogers
San Francisco

Editorial Director
Mary-Dawn Earley *Paris*

Managing Editor
Jane Fraser *San Francisco*

Consultant Editor
Joan Clibbon *London*

Editor
Beverley Barnes *Sydney*

Production Directors
Stephanie Sherman
 San Francisco
Mick Bagnato *Sydney*

Author
Jan Morris *Gwynedd, Wales*

**Caption and Additional
Text Author**
Roger Williams *London*

Art Director
Michael Rand *London*

Design Coordinator
Suzanne Hodgart *London*

Designer
Ian Denning *London*

Photographers
Torbjörn Andersson *Sweden*
Yann Arthus-Bertrand *France*
Max Dereta *Netherlands*
Georg Gerster *Switzerland*
Leo Meier *Switzerland*
Oddbjörn Monsen *Norway*
Horst Munzig *Germany*
Daniel Philippe *Belgium*
Georg Riha *Austria*
Guido Alberto Rossi *Italy*
Michael St Maur Sheil
 United Kingdom
Emil Schulthess *Switzerland*
Thomas Stephan *Germany*
Adam Woolfitt *United Kingdom*

Pilots
Apolinar Costas Alonso *Spain*
Captain Enzo Bianchini
 Italy and Greece
Peter Bakonyi *Hungary*
Ivan Chabonov *Bulgaria*
Bo Conneryd *Sweden*
Steve Diapér *Sweden*
Stig Ekdahl *Sweden*
Pelle Ericson *Sweden*
Bengt Follinge *Sweden*

Jonas Friedman *Sweden*
Kurt Friess *Germany*
Bjorn Gillberg *Sweden*
Bernhard Huschle *Germany*
Reinhold Immler *Germany*
Otokar Josefcak *Germany*
Janos Kécsán *Hungary*
Jan Koster *Netherlands*
Mats Ling *Sweden*
Nemesio Cubedo Machado
 Spain
Jonas Moell *Sweden*
Jan Narlinge *Sweden*
Ulf Nasstrom *Sweden*
Vujosevich Radoslave
 Yugoslavia
Rals Ralnrotteen *Germany*
Wolfgang Retzbach *Germany*
Bjorn Sundtrom *Sweden*
Robert Reutter *Luxembourg*
Ralf Rottgen *Germany*
Phillip Sheldon
 United Kingdom
Peter Szczepanski *Poland*
Tore Wolff *Norway*
Xavier Zorilla *Spain*
Sañarari Zoltan *Hungary*

Copyright © 1998 Weldon Owen Inc.
Weldon Owen Inc.
814 Montgomery Street,
San Francisco, CA 94133
Telephone: (415) 291-0100
Fax: (415) 291-8841

ISBN 1-887451-20-X

Printed in China by Toppan Printing Co.

MICHAEL YAMASHITA

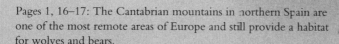

Blimp Team
Andreas Erd *London*
Manfred Kalina *Vienna*
Oliver Koehler *London*
Vincent Page *London*
Georg Riha *Vienna*
Arno Sammer *Vienna*
Glynis Watts *London*

Special Consultants

Design
John Bull, The Book Design
  Company *Sydney*

Production
Norman de Brackinghe
  Hong Kong

Eastern Europe Liaison
Malcolm Fudge *London*

European Co-publishing
Didier Millet *Paris*

Editorial and Photographic Researchers
Hans Christian Adam
  Germany
Emilia Chivu *Romania*
Salvatore di Napoli *France*
Michal Donath
  Czechoslovakia
John Falconer *England*
Urszula Hooker *Poland*
Marita Kankowski-Senfft
  Germany
Vincent Page *England*
Candace Roper *France*
Camilla Sardell *France*
Muk Swart *Netherlands*
Douglas Tunstell *Portugal*
Vibor Mulic *Poland*

Map Illustrations
Swanston Graphics
  Leeds, England

Weldon Owen

Chairman
Kevin Weldon *Sydney*

President
John Owen *San Francisco*

Marketing Director
Dawn Low *San Francisco*

General Manager
Stuart Laurence *Sydney*

Co-Editions Director
Derek Barton *Sydney*

Financial Director
Stanley Chan *Sydney*

Finance Manager
Richard VanOosterhout
  San Francisco

Administrative Managers
Beverley Sharpe *Sydney*
Sigrid Chase *San Francisco*

Administrative Assistants
Katharina Vitols *Sydney*
Amy Morton *San Francisco*

Administrative Accountants
Tony Badaoui *Sydney*
Fee-Ling Tan *San Francisco*

Production Assistant
Simone Perryman *Sydney*

Editorial Assistants
Sharon Freed *Sydney*
Ruth Jacobson *San Francisco*
Valérie Millet *San Francisco*

Pages 1, 16–17: The Cantabrian mountains in northern Spain are one of the most remote areas of Europe and still provide a habitat for wolves and bears.

Pages 2–3: Our Lady of the Rocks, built in the sixteenth century, stands on a man-made island in the Bay of Kotor, south of Dubrovnik, Yugoslavia. Sailors heaped stones and boulders onto a reef here until it was solid enough to sustain the building of a church.

Pages 4–5: Built in the 1890s, these rows of houses in Østerbro, Copenhagen, Denmark are called Kartoffelraekkerne (potato rows) or English style, referring to the acres of terraced housing that went up around the industrial cities of England in the nineteenth century.

Pages 6–7: The River Arno in Florence, Italy, has flooded several times with devastating results, most recently in 1966. After a flood in 1345 Ponte Vecchio, the old bridge, was rebuilt in its present shape, probably by the painter Taddeo Gaddi.

Pages 8–9: The roofs were taken off Fountains Abbey in 1539 on the orders of Henry VIII during the dissolution of England's monasteries. Since then it has gracefully decayed.

Pages 12–13: Every day during the July festival of San Fermín in Pamplona, Spain, the *encierro*, or running of the bulls, is followed by a separate event in the bullring.

Pages 14–15: Mariacki Church in Kraków, Poland, is in the northeast corner of the magnificent square built around the Sukiennice, the old cloth hall. Developed from a regular open market and rebuilt in 1555, it still has market stalls.

Pages 16–17 Small Photos (top to bottom):
Guido Alberto Rossi; Adam Woolfitt; Oddbjørn Monsen; Thomas Stephan; Georg Gerster; Georg Gerster; Guido Alberto Rossi

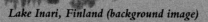

Lake Inari, Finland (background image)

Way up in the north of Finland, on the edge of Norway and the Soviet Union, is Inari, a lake as big as an inland sea. Some 3000 islands are scattered around its clear, still waters, and until the last century they were used by the Lapps as burial places: only here were the departed safe from hungry bears.

Endpapers: Satellite mosaic of Europe, National Remote Sensing Centre, Farnborough, United Kingdom

CONTENTS

THE LATINS *35*

Italy Spain Portugal France Malta

THE ISLANDERS *105*

United Kingdom Republic of Ireland

THE NORTHERNERS *135*

Sweden Norway Denmark Finland Iceland

GEORG GERSTER

PROLOGUE

Here stand I, almost at the end of the twentieth century, a Welsh European! Not for nearly 2000 years, since the days of the Roman Empire, has anyone in my small and drizzly homeland been able to make such a claim. A European! People could be Danish, Irish, Sicilian, Lapp, Belgian, Austrian, Welsh or Ruritanian, but until recently it was impossible for any of us seriously to think of ourselves as citizens of Europe. We were not Europeans as others were Chinese or Americans. We shared no collective purpose or conscience. Europe was not an object of loyalty, only a geographical definition, and the notion of European unity seemed a pipedream or an absurdity – or a nightmare, for only conquerors had ever seemed likely to achieve it.

It is true that in the past Europeans often felt themselves integrated by a common superiority to the rest of the world – by the fact of their civilization, which was to them the *only* civilization. Europeans meeting in distant parts would greet each other as comrades. As the French navigator La Pérouse observed, when he arrived uninvited and not much wanted at the infant British settlement on Botany Bay, Australia, 'all Europeans are countrymen at such a distance from home'. Edward Gibbon, the eighteenth-century historian, thought there was in fact a kind of European republic, permanently in alliance against 'the savage nations of the world'. There was, however, no real sense of commonality to these sentiments. Gibbon's republic was a scholar's fancy; French and English might be polite to each other on the other side of the world, but would be at each others' throats at home.

In our own time, indeed, Europe has seemed less a unity than ever. The figurative Iron Curtain between communism and capitalism was apparently indestructible, and made one half of the continent feel permanently estranged from the other. To travel from Brussels to Bucharest at the height of the ideological Cold War was an almost medieval experience, enveloped as one was in hostile bureaucracy, often spied upon, subjected to perpetual propaganda and sometimes very frightened. It was less of a culture shock to go to Cairo or Tokyo.

Now the Curtain has dissolved, and the concept of being European has acquired a new validity. The existence of this book, like my proud cry from the Celtic fringe, testifies to a grand development: the emergence of a Europe that can dimly be discerned, by optimists at least, as a true community. Never since the legions left Caernarfon has a citizen of Wales been able to proclaim herself a citizen of Europe too; never before has it been possible for photographers to portray from the air the whole of this endemically divided and suspicious continent. We are historical symptoms, the book and I. We are the flotsam of a high spring tide.

When the legions withdrew, and Europe fell apart again, this shaky sense of identity was not exactly lost, but was kept in abeyance. The nation-State was born, and for hundreds of years the kingdoms, principalities and republics of Europe fought each other for supremacy or survival, inflamed by dynastic jealousies, or border disputes, or the grievance of minorities, or water rights, or simply relative grandeurs. As the American poet Ogden Nash scoffed:

and so it goes for ages and aeons,
between these neighboring Europeans.

A telling memorial to these tragic futilities is the runic inscription carved on the flank of a stone lion at Venice. It records the participation of mercenary soldiers from Scandinavia, at one extremity of Europe, at the behest of the Byzantine Emperor of Constantinople, at another, in a punitive expedition to Greece. The lion, itself brought to Venice as war booty from the Piraeus, looks rather sheepish to be bearing this message of wasted belligerence, and indeed nothing could be much sillier than the history of Europe between the fall of Rome and the end of the Cold War. Some twenty-eight separate sovereignties still govern this corner of the world: it is only now – and perhaps only briefly now – that we are once more able to contemplate it as a putative unity, and to view the whole of it from the skies above without being shot down by missiles.

Another poignant illustration of European fatuity is provided by Vienna, the capital of Austria. Indisputably one of the world's supreme cities, haunted by the shades of its celebrated citizens and majestic with official buildings, today Vienna is a political absurdity. A quarter of all the Austrians live within the city limits, and the writ of those mighty offices of State, portentous beneath their emblems of old consequence, in fact runs hardly more than a couple of hundred miles in any direction.

This is a very European phenomenon. It arises in Vienna because this was once the capital of a much wider dominion – nothing less than the great Empire of the Habsburgs, which ruled half Europe. In those days Vienna's talent for pomp, its instinct for hierarchy, the seductive rhythm of its waltzes, the arias of its operas, set the criteria of civilized life for millions of Austrians, Hungarians, Bulgarians, Yugoslavs and Romanians, and to countless citizens it seemed the centre of all things. The history that has shrivelled it into impotence has had similar effects all over Europe, causing cities, provinces, kingdoms and republics to rise and fall and sometimes rise again, and often throwing whole generations confusingly out of one nationality into another.

The continent is entangled in a web of frontiers. Some of its borders are geographically obvious: the Rhine is one, the English Channel another, the Danube conveniently separates Bulgaria from Romania, the Pyrenees properly divide Spain from France, the summit of the Matterhorn is as good a place as anywhere to draw a line between Italy and Switzerland. More often, though, the logic of the frontiers is blurred, and queer anomalies abound. The Channel Islands, close to the coast of France, are British. Rhodes, near the coast of Turkey, is Greek. Gibraltar, which forms the southern tip of Spain, owes its allegiance to the Queen of England, while Llivia, within the French region of Roussillon, is subject to the King of Spain. Some states contain populations speaking several languages – in France alone eight are spoken. Some populations have been repeatedly tossed back and forth between different States. Preposterous corridors have been decreed to link detached possessions of the same sovereignty, and a place like Trieste has been so confused by the exchanges of history that a stranger arriving there uninformed could hardly guess what country he was in. On the map the frontiers of Europe often look like the meandering doodles of statesmen, idling away the hours of a conference, and perhaps that is what they sometimes are.

Yet with frontiers, however artificial, goes patriotism. Patriotism has been at once the glory and the disgrace of Europe, and you feel its ambiguous energy wherever you go. It is not an innocuous pride in the beauty of a countryside, the success of an economic system, the glory of a history, the splendour of a literature. More often it is the stirring but irrational devotion to a State – a particular patch of territory, enclosed within man-made limits and taught to think of itself as different from all others. Part of the thrill of Europe is its effulgence of nationalistic display. It is hard not to feel a frisson of Frenchness, for instance, if you should ever stride down the Champs-Elysées in Paris on a public holiday, when the traffic is cleared, the flags are flying, and you can march towards the Arc de Triomphe feeling like de Gaulle himself. But it is an illicit thrill, for more than anything else the chauvinist love of country has brought this continent into disrepute, besides slaughtering its peoples by the million and cruelly delaying its fulfilment.

Every degree of State flourishes in Europe, and demands its own allegiance. In and among the great kingdoms and republics are many semi-States hardly less proud of their dignities. Liechtenstein and Monaco, Andorra and San Marino and the Vatican are all States of a kind, with their own stamps and currencies, their own laws and their own ceremonial figureheads – a Prince, a Grand Duke, a pair of State Presidents or a Pope. And far fiercer still can be patriotism among those nations of Europe that are not States at all, but have long been forcibly subsumed into greater political entities. Hardly a week goes by, even in the 1990s, without the explosion of a bomb among the Basques, an ethnic fracas in Yugoslavia, the burning of an English-owned cottage by the Welsh or some act of

Hvězda Summer Castle, Prague, Czechoslovakia

Prague's Royal Game Reserve was founded at Bilá Hora (White Mountain) by Ferdinand I in 1534. Some 24 years later his son, Archduke Ferdinand of Tyrol, designed this three-storey hunting lodge, the Hvězda Summer Castle. Today it is a museum for the works of writer Alois Jirásek and painter Mikoláš Aleš.

Cologne Cathedral, Cologne, Germany

The dazzling cathedral in Cologne, as intricate as filigrees and
shining like scrubbed gold, sweeps up from the Domplatz, proud
to be the largest Gothic building in all Germany. Its cornerstone
was laid in 1248 around relics of the Magi, but work was halted
after it was only partially built. Work began again in the nineteenth
century, particularly on this west front, using original medieval
plans. It was finally completed in 1880, 632 years after it was begun.

nationalist vendetta in Corsica. These passionate struggles are like after-quakes, as it were,
to the terrible seismic convulsions that created modern Europe.

Europe has been a magnet and an epitome. It has drawn multitudes of pilgrims to its
shrines, and not a few predators to its riches. Neolithics apart, all its original inhabitants
came originally from somewhere else, and even within historic times alien peoples have
repeatedly threatened to master it. In the thirteenth century the Mongols, storming out
of the Asian heartlands, advanced far into Poland and Hungary and seemed likely for a time
to swarm across the entire continent. In the fifteenth century the Muslim Turks seized the
Byzantine capital of Constantinople and established an Islamic foothold in western Europe
which still survives. And in the eighth century the Arabs and Berbers had come out of
Africa to create, in one corner of Europe, an historical allegory.

The Muslim Moors ruled much of Spain for seven centuries, and would perhaps have
ruled France too if they had not been defeated in 732 AD, near Poitiers, in one of the crucial

battles of all history. By the end of the fifteenth century they were out of Spain, out of Europe altogether, but they left behind tantalizing relics of the synthesis they had achieved during their long presence. It is an ironic truth that of all the cultures of Europe, the forcibly imposed culture of the alien Moors, blended so anomalously with the Spanish genius, remains in the historical memory the most suggestively serene – rich in sciences and philosophies, full of poetry and delight, expressing itself in gardens and golden buildings that remain today, absorbed into the harsher beauties of Christian Spain, poignant images of a Golden Age. Perhaps it never really was one, but still I never travel among these enchanted memorials without imagining what Europe might have been, if it had been less haughty in its generations, and more relaxed.

For there is no pretending that serenity has been a European characteristic. This is a place of conflict. There are few cities in the continent that have not, at one time or another, been razed, looted, fought over or bombed; and deep in the collective unconscious of Europe is a sceptical distrust of destiny.

The rivalries and ambitions of Europe have embroiled the whole world. An obscure assassin kills an Austrian aristocrat in a small town in the Balkans, and within a couple of years men are slaughtering each other in East Africa, in Iraq or in the Indian Ocean. A demagogue comes to power in Germany, and twelve years later the nuclear bomb falls on Japan. The plagues of Europe become the curses of humanity, and in our own time Europe's mass murder of its Jews has come to seem a very paradigm of suffering itself. This continent has more often had cause to weep than to celebrate, and the lovely landscapes that are spread through the pages of this book are soaked in blood and tears.

Yet the Europeans long thought themselves the arbiters of right and wrong, with licence to command all lesser breeds. In the Middle Ages the Pope had no qualms about dividing the unexplored world between Spain and Portugal. A century ago Europe thought it perfectly proper to seize huge slabs of other continents, declaring their inhabitants subject to itself, and exploiting their resources for its own aggrandizement. A vast aggressive energy emanated from Europe for a thousand years and more, and at one time or another European Powers ruled the entire African continent, the whole of India, all the Americas and everything there was in Australasia.

In particular the forceful seaboard Powers of western Europe projected their values and manners across half the world. The Spaniards contemptuously swept away the Inca and the Aztec civilizations. The French established their *lycées* from Indo-China to the Caribbean. The Portuguese declared themselves rightful landlords of Brazil. The Dutch commanded an enormous empire in the eastern seas. Even the Danes acquired enclaves in India, and the British sailed out from their petty islands to rule nearly a quarter of the earth's landmass and govern, uninvited, a quarter of all its inhabitants. English, French and Spanish became world languages. European systems of law, education, religion and technique were distributed among baffled indigenes in improbable environments. It became a military commonplace to find soldiers marching in turbans, coolie hats and flowing robes beneath a tricolour or a Union Jack.

Europe, that peninsula of Asia, dominated the world. More important still, it created new worlds of its own. The empires presently retreated as the twentieth century re-ordered matters, but the irreversible victory of Europe was this: that throughout North America and in the distant territories of Australasia, sovereign settlements of Europeans were there to stay. Great new nations grew up in Europe's image far away, and the balance of the world was permanently affected. Imagine a United States founded by Asians, say, or an Australia by Africans, and you may realize how fateful have been the results of this particular continent's imperial urges. When in the 1960s the Common Market came into existence in western Europe, people in New Zealand, on the other side of the globe, felt quite disgruntled to be excluded from it.

The personality of Europe is kaleidoscopic, moulded by different national origins, rooted in thousands of regional customs and references, embodied in disparate cultures and sealed by the effects of countless wars. Yet there is some abstraction, more than mere geography, which does bind this extraordinary gallimaufry into a whole. Even Europe's most blazing nationalists would probably admit to its existence, and recognize the power of the European identity.

Gibbon defined it as a 'system of arts, and laws and manners', but I think it some more metaphysical arrangement. Perhaps it is partly the bond of shared experience. To one degree or another every European people shares a history. We have mostly fought the same wars, on one side or another. We have endured similar political or ideological processes. Common depressions and catastrophes have oppressed us, and common tyrants have bullied us. The wind makes people in Ireland shiver as they shiver on the Polish plains, and when the Chernobyl reactor blew up it polluted both the vineyards of Bulgaria and the sheep-farms of Wales.

But more probably Europe's identity is a matter of theory. The continent is built upon an immense foundation of very old theories, and one in particular used to be synonymous with Europeanness. The spark of Christianity came from the east, of course, but it was Europe that fanned it into flame, and here the Christian faith was formalized, institutionalized, intellectualized and popularized. It is true that even within the faith the

Europeans continued to quarrel – the Reformation which split the continent in the sixteenth century reverberates still on Europe's western fringe, where the Catholics and Protestants of Ireland are locked in apparently insoluble conflict. Nevertheless the notion of Christianity has surely been the greatest of all the factors that have distinguished Europe from its neighbour continents. The first pan-European armies were the armies of the Christian Crusades, and as often as not the European imperialists sailed out to conquer the world as missionaries of Christ. Europe is the world headquarters of Christianity still, and until recent years it could truly have been called a Christian continent. Only its Jewish

THOMAS STEPHAN

Småland, Sweden

Harvest time in Småland, southern Sweden, where the hay is kept dry in plastic wrapping. The region looks prosperous now, but in the nineteenth century poor agriculture and a booming population meant Småland accounted for a fifth of Sweden's one million emigrants to the United States. At the nearby town of Växjö there is a House of Emigrants which has a museum and the largest archives on the subject in Europe.

communities, the Muslims of its eastern marches and immigrants from elsewhere would have declared themselves anything else. To a visitor from Mars it might feel like one still. Half the pictures in this book, I would guess, include the tower or steeple of a Christian temple, and often the pattern of a city is built around its presence, just as the pattern of European history has so often been dictated by its passions.

Only in our century have the godless creeds of the Nazis and the Communists tried unsuccessfully to mould the continent in other spiritual kinds, and it is still some distillation of the Christian principle that gives these countries a degree of moral cohesion. That the majority of Europeans are now probably pagan or agnostic has not yet weakened this heritage, or turned its noble monuments into museums. If Europe's cathedrals are no longer declarations of the continent's creed, they still symbolize its identity.

During the past half-century Europe sometimes seems to have lost its dynamism, divided as it has been by ideologies, and generally playing a passive rather than active role in the world. It has fallen into what used to be called, in the days of the old empires, Spheres of Influence – American in the west, Soviet in the east. Japanese and Arab money has become indispensable, too, and in some parts of the continent millions of immigrants from elsewhere have changed the style of life.

Nevertheless one cannot take a journey across this continent, whether on land or in the air, without sensing the colossal latent power of it. Its 500 million inhabitants have survived all challenges and miseries to remain perhaps the most variously gifted and productive of all the world's peoples. The achievements of its past are stacked up, so to speak, like a reactor, and the energy of all its prodigies seems to irradiate it. Sophocles, Einstein, Tolstoy, Mozart, Palladio, Pasteur, Shakespeare, Michelangelo – the list is like a roster of human achievement itself. To think that one small continent (to parody the Irishman Oliver Goldsmith) could do so much!

Yet to be a European has not always been a source of pride. Americans and Australians have often thought it an effete or decadent condition. Activists of the Third World have thought it distinctly unwholesome. During the past couple of centuries, at least, Europe has given the rest of humankind as much tragedy as blessing, and nobody could boast of the continent's general behaviour in our own times – it could perhaps be said that of all man's inhumanities to man, the cruelties of Europe in the 1940s were the worst.

Time heals, though. We are learning slowly that it is States, not people, that really commit patriotic atrocities; and as the eventful twentieth century comes to a close, Europe seems at last half-reconciled to itself. The nations of the west, so long enemies, are slowly coalescing. The nations of the east, so long estranged, are beginning to see themselves once

Pátmos Island, Greece

For 300 years after the monastery of St John was built, no secular buildings were allowed on Pátmos, the smallest of Greece's Dodecanese islands near the coast of Turkey. It was founded in 1088 and dedicated to the Apostle St John, who supposedly wrote the Apocalypse in a nearby cave while in exile. The monastery was the object of Byzantine emperors' devotions, and it became rich and well endowed.

more as part of the European whole. Perhaps it will all go sour again, the Balkans will relapse into discord, the old enemies across the Rhine will again come to blows, the British will turn their backs on the continent and look to the sea once more. But at least we see in Europe today the hope of a peaceful continental community – a prospect nobody has been able to discern for a couple of thousand years.

This book is a visual record of all Europe at this fateful moment. It is the record of an ideal. Nobody but the gods and the angels has been able to see it like this before: the whole marvellous place, in all its diversity, surveyed at a divine remove from its squalors and squabbles. It is the nearest one can get to seeing Europe in the abstract, the idea of it rather than the muddied fact; and of course even now only the idea of it enables me, standing on my terrace in Gwynedd beside the Irish Sea, to look east across England, across the Netherlands, across Germany, across Poland, to the marches of Asia where the winds come from, and to feel myself exhilaratingly a member of it all – a European at last.

33

THE LATINS

ITALY SPAIN PORTUGAL FRANCE MALTA

I n the southwest of Europe, between the Adriatic Sea and the Atlantic Ocean, live the peoples commonly called Latins, stereotyped often as hot-blooded, romantic and artistic. In fact they are related more by the common Latin root of their languages than by anything else, and the five countries they inhabit are as ethnically complex as anywhere else on the continent. Greeks, Phoenicians, Celts, Arabs have all settled in these parts at one time or another, adding their own elements to the common stock, and by now a Sicilian, a Portuguese, a Milanese, an Andalusian and a Parisian would hardly recognize each other as fellow-Latins at all.

Geographically, too, the region is many-faced. Its southern shores are, of course, pure Mediterranean. These are the lands of the olives, the oranges, the perfumed shrubs and the scraggy goats, tinged by memories of classical Greece. The sea is not always as clear as it

---

Château de Chambord, Loire, France (left)

Walking along the balustraded promenade that encircles the Château de Chambord at just below roof level is like walking down a street – past doors and bay windows and beneath dormers, towers, lanterns and some of its 365 decorated chimneys.

Naples, Italy (previous pages)

Above the clamour of its lively streets, the city of Naples takes on an unexpectedly ordered air. The redbrick building in the centre is the Nunziatella Military College, and beyond it Castel dell'Ovo guards the harbour.

Gozo Island, Malta (above)

The island of Gozo is part of Malta, an arid archipelago between Sicily and North Africa, whose position at the centre of Mediterranean trading routes has made it one of the most important strategic places in the whole sea.

Gibraltar (right)

Gibraltar, claimed by Spain (from which it protrudes), is Britain's last outpost in Europe, just 2.5 square miles (6.5 square kilometres) in area. The concrete slope on the east side of the Rock is designed to collect water.

used to be, the beaches are often hideously developed, but still over much of these coasts there hangs an almost palpable suggestion of myth. Corsica, the greatest island of the region, is clad with the aromatic *maquis*, the tangle of thyme, oleander, lavender, mint and myrtle that gave its name to the French resistance movement of the Second World War.

Inland from the coasts, however, the numen hardens. Only 40 miles (65 kilometres) from the pleasure-beaches of Spain rise the Sierra Nevada highlands, whose topmost villages are the highest in Europe, and beyond that again stands the bitter and terrific plateau of Castile, full of castles and formidable towns. The coasts of Italy may be benign, but the spine of the country is the severe range of the Apennines, interspersed by a thousand rugged valleys, patched with dark forests and still inhabited, here and there, by wolves. Portugal does not have a Mediterranean coast at all and faces only the stern Atlantic. As for France, which Winston Churchill once called the fairest portion of the earth's surface, it stretches away from the warm Provençal hills above the sea to fetch up on the chill sand-dunes of the English Channel, about as far from the Mediterranean ethos as one could get.

Yet history has made, if not a family of these States, at least an association. In particular it was here, in the swathe of territories that lay in the lee of the Alps, that Christianity, the chief coalescing force of Europe, developed its power and its aesthetic. From the village

38

La Défense, Paris, France (left)

The Arc de Triomphe has the
biggest picture frame in the world.
The Grand Arch at La Défense,
one of Paris's monumental
buildings of the 1980s, rises in
the west of the city where it is a
window on the modern finance
and business district. Designed by
Johan Otto von Spreckelsen, it is
361 feet (110 metres) high and
328 feet (100 metres) wide.

Monte Carlo, Monaco (right)

Many have tried in vain to break
the bank beneath the roofs of the
casino at Monte Carlo. The first
casino in Monaco was built in
1856 to give the ruling prince an
income. This one was built
between 1878 and 1910, and for
years it was the main source of
revenue for the principality.

DANIEL PHILIPPE

churches of Malta to the immense and marvellous cathedrals of Spain and France, from
lonely mountain shrines to the Vatican itself at the centre of it all, the old consequence of
this faith proclaims itself here as nowhere else.

Here too exploded the Renaissance, that surge of all the arts and sciences which was
at once to challenge and glorify the Christian creed, and which now makes all Europe a
treasure-house of its artifacts. Much of the artistic genius of Europe has come from this
corner of it, much of the philosophical and scientific genius too. The navigators of
Portugal and Spain opened the rest of the world to European exploration, creating the first
of the great maritime empires of history; later the French flag too would fly over colonies
across the world; and almost until the last gasp of the imperial age Italy was still collecting
territories overseas.

From minute Malta, then, to majestic France, a congeries of peoples astonishingly
inventive and adventurous. Today France, Spain and Italy are three of the chief industrial
States of Europe, while Portugal remains agricultural, and the Republic of Malta, whose
385 000 people speak a language derived partly from Italian, partly from Arabic, stands as
a reminder that wherever we are on Europe's southern shores, we are never far from Africa.
Here two worlds are linked – the warm cherishing south, the hard and thrusting north
– and their mingled meanings contribute powerfully to the personality of Europe.

Perugia, Italy

The top of a pie smoothed flat by the back of a fork would look like this church roof in Perugia. As ageless as the earth, Roman tiles have given the whole Mediterranean its architectural flavour. These belong to Sant'Angelo, one of Europe's earliest churches, founded in the fifth century as the glory of the Roman Empire was crumbling into history. Before then on this site in this former Etruscan city, there was a temple to other gods.

GUIDO ALBERTO ROSSI

GUIDO ALBERTO ROSSI

Adriatic Riviera, Italy (left)

From high above, the serried ranks of umbrellas look like a strip of needlepoint. They could be anywhere along the Adriatic Riviera, northeastern Italy's popular playground. The 75 miles (120 kilometres) of lidos and hotel complexes stretch from the River Po south to Cattolica. The river's silt accounts for the sandy beaches and has left the port of Adria, which gave the Adriatic its name, several miles inland.

Santa Maria della Salute, Venice, Italy (above)

As a thanksgiving for deliverance from the plague in 1660, the Senate in Venice ordered the building of Santa Maria della Salute beside the Grand Canal. Next to the basilica is the Patriarchal Seminary, and on the left of the geometrically patterned pavement are the seventeenth-century customs sheds.

Venice, Italy (overleaf)

The sun shines on Venice, Queen of the Adriatic, lighting her palaces, piazzas and domes. In the centre is the campanile of St Mark's. The Doge's Palace stretches along to the waterfront, where it looks out at the island of San Giorgio Maggiore. The Grand Canal begins at the triangular customs house by the pearl-white church of Santa Maria della Salute.

GUIDO ALBERTO ROSSI

Stromboli, Italy (above)

About 400 people live on this constantly active volcanic
cone. Known as The Black Giant, Stromboli is the most
northerly of the seven Lipari islands to the north of Sicily
and west of Italy's toe. The rumbles are ceaseless, and the
eruptions light the night sky and pour glowing lava into
the sea.

Pompeii, Italy (right)

Until 24 August AD 79, Pompeii was a bustling place of
shops, bars and taverns. Its main road, Via di Stabia (seen
here), led to the sunny colonnaded marketplace. But
when Vesuvius's volcano erupted on that summer's day,
the town and one-tenth of its 20000 citizens were buried
in lava and ash.

The Colosseum, Rome, Italy (overleaf)

The whole panoply of Rome's
empire is evoked in the
Colosseum. The Eternal City's
most enduring monument, built
for the first plebeian emperor,
Vespasian, was inaugurated in
AD 80. On the first day 5000 wild
animals were killed to amuse the
spectators. The building was faced
with marble and stucco, and
awnings kept the sun from the
audience's critical eyes.

48

GUIDO ALBERTO ROSSI

Campo dei Fiori, Rome, Italy (left)

In the warm morning sunlight, the shouts of the street sellers and the aroma of their produce drift up from Campo dei Fiori in an artisan quarter of Rome. For more than a century a daily market has been held in this 'Field of Flowers', brightened by colourful umbrellas and shades. In sombre contrast is the bronze statue in its midst. It is of Giordano Bruno, the philosopher, who was burned here in 1600 after a seven-year trial by the Inquisition.

Victor Emmanuel Monument, Rome, Italy (right)

The Victor Emmanuel Monument is a triumph of 'wedding cake' architecture, although Italians may refer to it as 'the big ricotta cake'. This great slab of Brescia marble was put up in the middle of Rome between 1885 and 1911 to celebrate the unification of Italy in 1861, when Victor Emmanuel II of Sardinia was made the country's first king.

St Peter's, Vatican City (overleaf)

At the heart of Christendom is this embrace (some say the claw) of the Church of Rome. Built with 284 columns and 88 pilasters and watched over by 96 martyrs and saints, the colonnades of Gianlorenzo Bernini's seventeenth-century Piazza San Pietro reach out from the great basilica of St Peter's, the greatest Renaissance church and centrepiece of the Vatican's 500-acre sovereign state.

GUIDO ALBERTO ROSSI

GUIDO ALBERTO ROSSI

Central Station, Milan, Italy (above)

For decades Milan, Italy's main commercial city, has been the place that sets the style. Many who come to see its fashion and fairs arrive here at the central station, designed by Ulisse Stracchini and completed in 1931. Giovanni Ponti designed the skyscraper in the foreground for the Pirelli tyre company in the 1950s.

The Duomo, Milan, Italy (right)

An 'imitation hedgehog' is how the English novelist D.H. Lawrence described the Duomo in Milan. At the heart of the city it is one of Europe's largest churches, and was founded with the gift of a marble quarry, which it has kept. The stone has been sculpted into some 2250 statues to add to the 135 pinnacles. The cathedral inspired builders for nearly 500 years, starting in 1386.

San Gimignano, Italy (previous pages)

The 13 skyscrapers of San Gimignano in Tuscany are all that remain of no less than 76 which grew out of this wealthy medieval town. Families built them so they could hurl stones down on their enemies, and to show off, they tried to top their neighbours' towers. Finally, the authorities, fearful that the People's Palace (in the centre of the photograph) might itself be surpassed, restricted their height to 177 feet (54 metres).

Siena, Italy (left)

Perhaps it is because
Siena gave the world
its name for the colour
of its rich Tuscan
earth, that its cathedral
seems so unexpectedly
bright. Made of green,
pink and white marble,
it was an early Gothic
church, built by 1215
and famous for its
statuary. Beyond it is
the Campo, a fan-shaped
square looked down on
by the thin, crenellated
fourteenth-century
Torre del Mangia
(wastrel tower). Twice
a year the square is filled
with a flag-waving
medieval pageant, which
climaxes in the furious
Palio horse race.

Pisa, Italy (right)

Seen from here, all the
buildings in Pisa's Campo
dei Miracoli (Field of
Miracles) seem slightly
askew. In the foreground
is the circular baptistery
and behind it the
beautiful white marble
Duomo. This illusion is
no doubt caused by the
'Leaning Tower', which
even now moves one-
twentieth of an inch
(1.19 millimetres) a year.

Camogli, Italy (previous pages)

Grey rocks, a grey beach and grey slated roofs on square housing blocks
fail to make Camogli, on the Riviera di Levante, look dull. Perhaps
it is the splash of colour from the boats and the warmth of the ochre-
coloured walls that give this hillside port, once famous for building
merchant ships, sufficient charm to attract holidaymakers.

62

The Meseta, Spain

These are the last southern acres of the Meseta, the great dry plateau that occupies more than half of Spain. At its centre is Madrid, 2100 feet (640 metres) above sea level. South of the capital the red-earth farmlands roll on mile after mile until they reach the wide, sparsely populated Sierra Morena, rising in the distance. This mountain chain stretches 300 miles (500 kilometres) from the Portuguese border to Albacete and cuts off the coastal region of Andalucía from the rest of Spain.

Madrid, Spain (overleaf)

Madrid's Las Ventas, a 1929 Mudejar-style building, is one of the country's leading bull-fighting arenas. *Corridas* are held from March to October, beginning at 5 pm when some of the heat has gone from the day; cheap seats are in the sun, more expensive ones in the shade. Each event involves three matadors who draw lots in the morning to see which of six bulls they will fight. A resident surgeon and modern infirmary reduce the likelihood of fatalities among the toreadors.

GEORG GERSTER

64

GEORG GERSTER

Consuegra, Spain (right)

The windmills of La
Mancha became
celebrated when the hero
of Miguel de Cervantes'
novel, *Don Quixote*, tilted
at them with his lance,
mistaking their sails for
the flailing arms of a giant.
They were a new device
then, introduced from the
Low Countries in about
1580, some 20 years
before the book was
published. Hundreds were
built, but only a few have
survived. In Consuegra
there are 13. Its castle,
which has Roman
foundations, belonged
to the Order of St John.

Santiago de Compostela, Spain (above)

In AD 813 a star pointed down on this spot in a field to show where
the remains of the Apostle St James could be found. Santiago de
Compostela, in northwest Spain, has been one of Europe's principal
sites of pilgrimage ever since. The cathedral dates from 1060–1211,
and its Baroque exterior was added in about 1740.

68

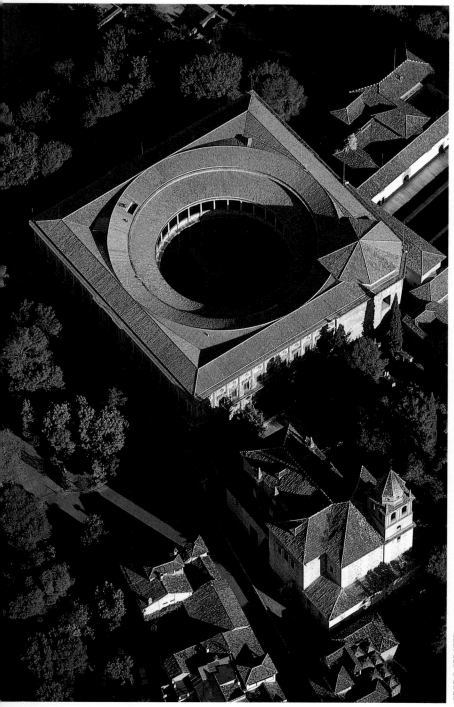

GEORG GERSTER

GEORG GERSTER

The Alhambra, Granada, Spain

A simple geometric roof covers the Palace of
Charles V, a late addition to the Alhambra, one
of the most exquisite complexes of buildings in
Europe. The Al Qal'a al-Hambra (the Red Fort)
was the hub of the Moorish kingdom of Granada
established in 1238. After the reconquest in
1492 the Spanish monarchs Ferdinand and Isabella
lived here for a while, appreciating its beauty.
'They lack our faith,' wrote the bishop of Córdoba
of the vanquished Muslims, 'but we their work.'

Plaza Mayor, Madrid, Spain

Perhaps it is the unbroken roof line as much as
the flat expanse of cobbled square that makes the
Plaza Mayor in Madrid look as if it has been
superimposed on the city. Building was started
not long after Philip II moved the royal court
here from Toledo in 1561. Subsequent monarchs
occupied apartments above the town bakery,
giving them a ringside view of the duelling,
jousting, bull baiting and heretic burning which
used to enliven the square.

70

Monasterio de San Lorenzo de El Escorial, Spain (overleaf)

Granite walls, grey-slated roofs, unexuberant solid symmetry . . . the largest building in Spain built by the most powerful ruler of his time is a perfect monument to the man. In 1563 the austere king Philip II had the Monasterio de San Lorenzo de El Escorial built in the Guadarrama Mountains northwest of Madrid. Part palace, part monastery, part mausoleum, it became the burial place for all but two subsequent monarchs.

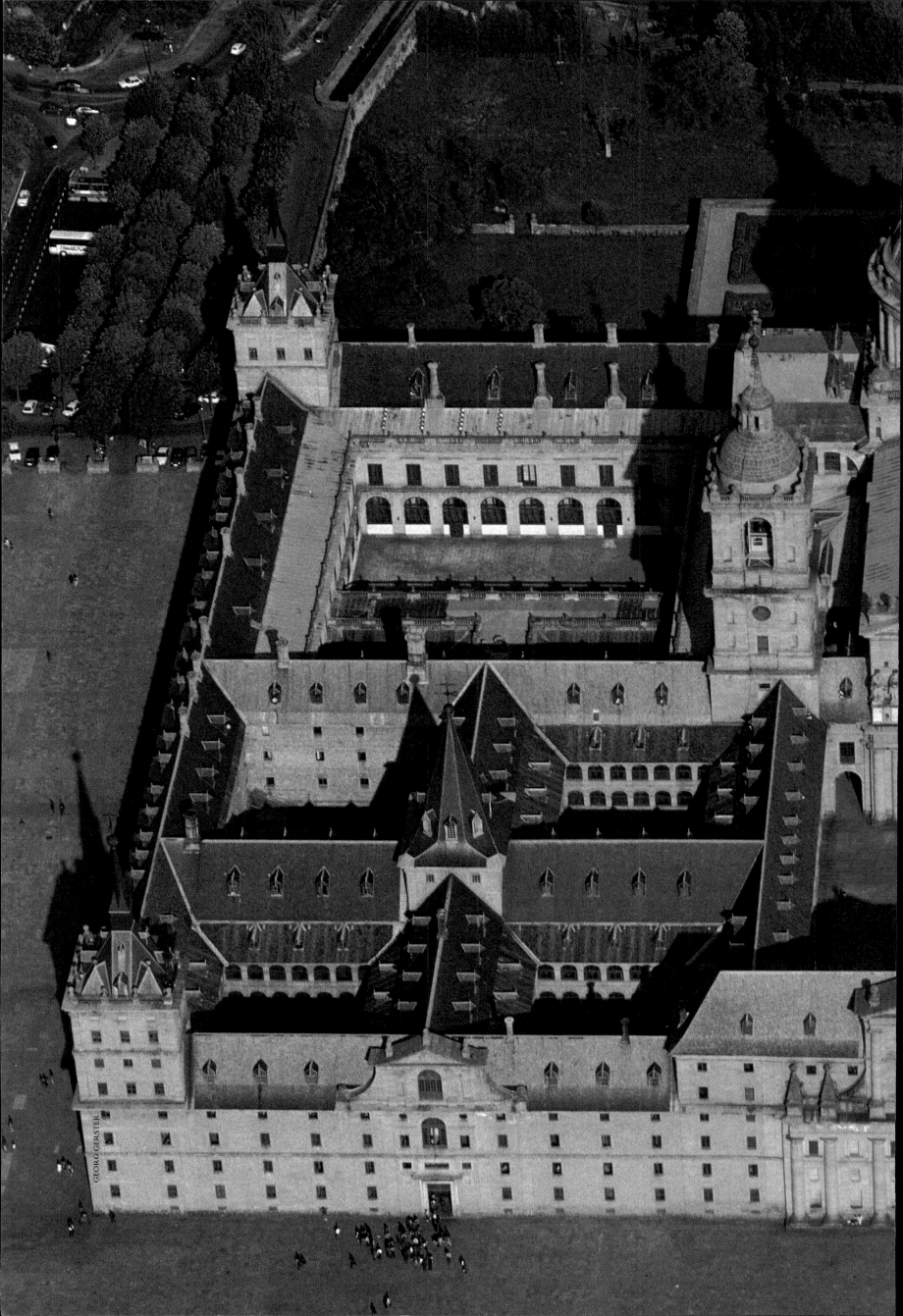

Pontevedra, Spain (previous pages)

Every year herds of wild horses are rounded up in the province of Pontevedra, northwest Spain. They are brought down from the Galician mountains to several towns, where they are marked and clipped, and it is always an occasion for celebration. Here, at Bayona-Oya, the 'round-up of the beasts' takes place on the second Sunday in June. Hair clipped from the horses' manes is sold to raise funds for the local church. The animals are afterwards returned to the hills to roam free.

Cádiz, Spain

When the Guadalquivir silted up in the eighteenth century Cádiz took over from Seville as southern Spain's principal port for Atlantic shipping. Trade with South America brought it temporary wealth which it expended, among other things, on its domed cathedral.

GEORG GERSTER

GEORG GERSTER

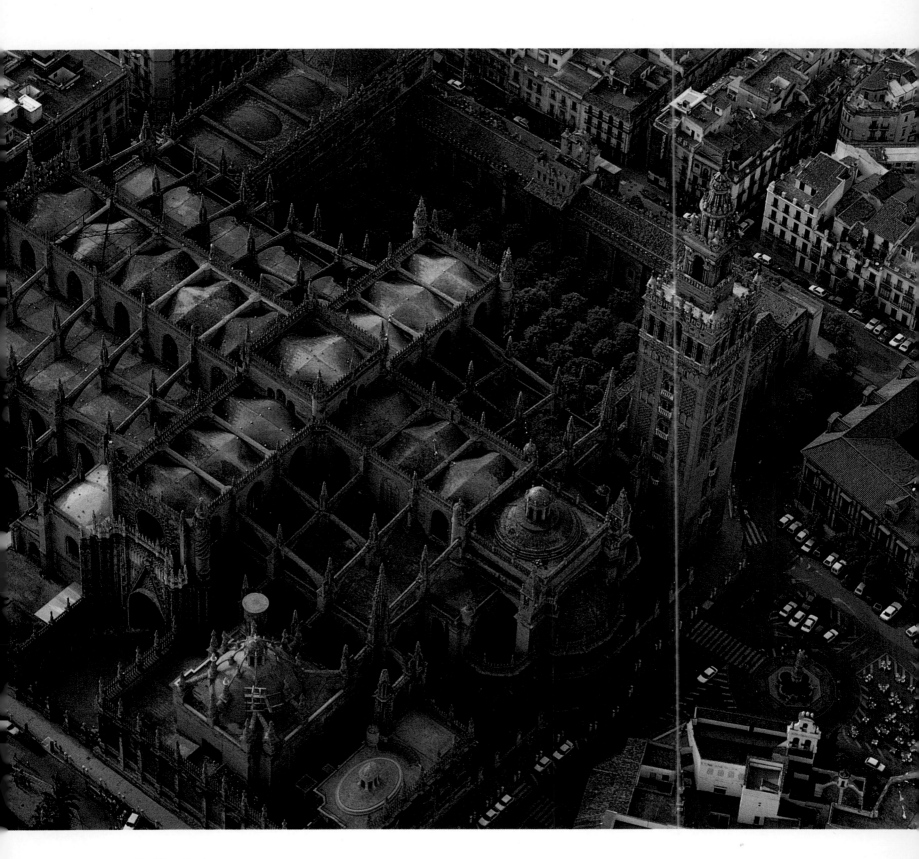

Seville, Spain

The immense size of the cathedral in Seville is not always appreciated but it is one of the largest in Christendom. It was built from 1401 to 1507 on the site of a mosque, which bequeathed its Patio de los Naranjos (Orange-Tree Courtyard), seen on the far side, and its minaret.

GEORG GERSTER

Marbella, Costa del Sol, Spain (above)

Just one more new development goes up near Marbella on the Costa del Sol, the southern coast of Spain. Developed steadily since the 1950s, the coast became fashionable in the 1970s oil crisis, when King Fahd of Saudi Arabia moved into a villa designed to resemble the White House.

Barcelona, Spain (right)

Barcelona's Expiatory Temple of the Holy Family, the Sagrada Família, seems to be as much a monument to its architect, Antoni Gaudí i Cornet, as it is to God. Gaudí worked on it from 1891 until his death in 1926, and he is buried in the crypt. Since then, the cathedral has come on in fits and starts. A local sculptor, Josep M. Subirachs, has embellished the near 'Passion' façade; a Japanese, Etsuro Sotoo, has added to the façade opposite.

Jerez de la Frontera, Spain (previous pages)

An artist could not have chosen a better shade of purple than this to flower against a silvery, parched vineyard near Jerez de la Frontera. Sherry has been made in this southwestern corner of Spain since the Middle Ages, dominated in recent times by dynastic families owning huge tracts of land. Modern business methods are changing their lifestyle, but local pure-bred Carthusian horses remain their passion.

GEORG GERSTER

Sintra, Portugal (left)

Pena Palace in Sintra near the Atlantic coast just above Lisbon is more used to looking down than being looked down upon. A convent was originally built here to celebrate the first sight of Vasco da Gama returning in 1499 from his pioneering voyage to India. The fantasy palace of the 1840s was designed by Baron Eschwege and built by Ferdinand of Saxe-Coburg-Gotha for his wife, Queen Maria II. He continued to live here with his second wife, a German singer, after the queen had died giving birth to their tenth child.

The Algarve, Portugal (above)

Eager to escape the regimentation of their uniformly workaday lives, holidaymakers from northern Europe, particularly Britain, have sought their dream villas in the Algarve, Portugal's southern shore. For 90 miles (145 kilometres), along a beautiful and once-impoverished coast, east and west of the town of Faro, there has been more tourist development than in the whole of the rest of the country put together. Here the desire seems to be unanimous: a blue pool, a patio, white walls, an ivory tower and red roof overhead.

83

Porto, Portugal

Porto, Portugal's second city, gave the name 'port' to its fortified wine and to the left-hand side of ships sailing south. The old town of narrow alleys, small bars and shops is on the north side of the River Douro. The vines are grown along the length of the river up to the border with Spain, and the wine used to be shipped down on sailing barges for export. Now the port houses are located in Gaia, on the south bank, reached by the two-tiered Dom Luis I Bridge.

GEORG GERSTER

GEORG GERSTER

Alentejo, Portugal

A lone farm building sits on one of many small hilltops among terraces of orchards, which pattern the landscape of lower Alentejo, southwest Portugal. The healthy soil here has brought settlers since the Romans. But profits from the land are not always attractive, especially when across the Serra de Monchique to the south lies the rich tourist industry of the Algarve.

**Château de Chaumont,
Loire, France**

Through the mists of time
comes the Château de
Chaumont. Among its
ghosts are Catherine de'
Medici, widow of Henri
II, and the writer Madame
de Staël, exiled here
from Paris by Napoléon.
In between, Benjamin
Franklin paid a visit, to
sit for an Italian sculptor
called Nini who had set
up a kiln in the stables to
produce medallions of the
famous. Approached across
a drawbridge, the château
has three wings. The
fourth side was pulled
down in 1739, opening up
a fine view (on a clear day)
over the Loire valley.

Paris, France (overleaf)

With Notre-Dame as its
wheelhouse, the Ile de la
Cité floats like a great
barge on the Seine
through the heart of Paris.
The twin-towered
cathedral was built
between 1163 and 1240,
and much of the rest of
the island is now
occupied by the Palais de
Justice. The near bank
(the 'Left Bank') is where
the city's colleges and
convents were founded.
Halfway up the picture on
the left is the Pompidou
Centre. In the foreground
is the sixteenth-century
Pont Neuf, which links
the island to the city's
two parts.

DANIEL PHILIPPE

YANN ARTHUS-BERTRAND/ALTITUDE

Burgundy, France (above)

Tending vines in Burgundy is an occupation that dates
back to Roman times. The Dukes of Burgundy used to
be called the 'Lords of the best wine in Christendom', and
their wines were served to popes and princes. Centred on
Côte de Nuits and Côte de Beaune, between Dijon and
Lyons, the vineyards are not large, and Burgundy's better-
known labels are among the most expensive in France.

Château de la Rochepot, Burgundy, France (right)

Flemish-style coloured glazed tiles are typical roof
decorations in the region of Burgundy, a reminder of the
time when the Duchy stretched into the Low Countries.
This is the castle at La Rochepot near Nolay just
southwest of Beaune, rebuilt in the fifteenth century on
an original twelfth-century castle.

Brittany, France (overleaf)

A lighthouse stands like a sentinel
on the Ile d'Ouessant, the most
westerly corner of France. Surging
around it are the waters of the
Atlantic as they approach the English
Channel. Frequently lashed by gales,
the island is known as Ushant in
English and Enez-Heussa (Terror
Island) to the Bretons. The islanders
live by fishing, and the women,
who by tradition make the proposals
of marriage, work the land.

DANIEL PHILIPPE

Vence, France (previous pages)

What drew Matisse, Picasso and
Rouault to the Côte d'Azur was
not just the blue sea, but the
medieval hilltop villages within
easy reach among the hills behind.
They all stayed here, in Vence,
between Nice and Antibes, though
they would never have had such a
view of it as this. At the centre, the
tower of the Romanesque church
stares up at the distant Alps, while
around it, like a great skirt, the
streets swirl in a giddy circle until
they reach the ravines at its sides.

Mont Louis, The Pyrenees, France (above)

In the decade from 1678, the French military engineer
Sébastien le Prestre de Vauban set about surrounding the
country with fortresses. This one at Mont Louis, in the
Pyrenees, is the highest garrison town in France. It
served as a frontier post against Spain, which had ceded
its territories north of the Pyrenees to France in 1659.

Haut-Koenigsbourg Castle, Alsace, France (right)

From its eyrie atop a 2485-foot (757-metre) hill, the
castle of Haut-Koenigsbourg has a spectacular view over
the plain of Alsace. Built in the twelfth century, it was
severely damaged in the Thirty Years War, and it
remained a ruin until 1901 when Alsace was for a time
part of Germany. Kaiser Wilhelm II then had it restored.

Château de Clermont, Loire, France (previous pages)

Château de Clermont is a privately-owned castle in the air. It is at Le Cellier in the Loire on the site of the former Chapel of Clermont and was built by René Chenu de Clermont in 1649. He was governor of two other châteaux, a minister for the prince of Condé and advisor to the king. His seigneurial rights at Le Cellier extended beyond the château to the surrounding villages. Life here was sufficiently exciting to attract the attention of the brilliant seventeenth-century writer Madame de Sévigné.

YANN ARTHUS-BERTRAND/ALTITUDE

DANIEL PHILIPPE

Mont Saint-Michel, Normandy, France

Mont Saint-Michel sits in so many empty miles of sand that it is easy to imagine the speed with which Europe's most powerful tide comes flooding in twice a day to surround it. A Benedictine monastery was founded on the 265-feet (80-metre) granite cone in the tenth century, and it became a place of pilgrimage, a fortress and, in the nineteenth century, a state prison. Now up to 6000 people cross the causeway each day to visit one of France's most popular sites.

St Malo, France

The nineteenth-century author Gustave Flaubert called this glittering
granite outcrop on the north coast of France 'a crown of stone above
the waves'. St Malo is a buccaneering port, built on booty looted from
shipping in the English Channel and elsewhere. Once an island, the
fortified old town was badly burned at the end of the Second World
War. Today, rebuilt, it is a popular resort. The islet just beyond
contains the tomb of the local writer Chateaubriand, 'Solitary in death
as he affected to be in life'.

THE ISLANDERS

UNITED KINGDOM
REPUBLIC OF IRELAND

Famously wet and windy between the North Sea and the Atlantic Ocean, the British Isles are perhaps the most fateful of all the world's islands, and they stand in a unique relationship to the rest of Europe. Four nations occupy these relatively uninviting islands – the English, the Irish, the Welsh and the Scots – and they are grouped into two States: 58 million people live in the United Kingdom of Great Britain and Northern Ireland, three and a half million live in the Republic of Ireland, and the mutual attitudes of the two are notoriously equivocal. The islands have not been occupied by an outside Power since 1066 AD, and for several centuries they have been governed, in one degree or another, by systems of parliamentary democracy.

Most of the land is good agricultural country, well-watered and easy. But in the west and in the north – in Wales, in much of Scotland, along the Atlantic shore of Ireland –

London, England, United Kingdom (left)

This is a familiar face of London: the clock above Westminster Palace, the seat of Britain's government since the eleventh century. From here the sound of the hour being struck by its largest bell, the 13½-ton (13.7-tonne) Big Ben, is deafening.

The South Downs, England, United Kingdom (previous pages)

The rolling chalk ridges of the South Downs come to an abrupt halt when they reach the English Channel around Eastbourne. The cliff faces show seven hills, divided by the valleys of former rivers, and known as the Seven Sisters.

107

Salisbury Plain, England, United Kingdom

There is a haunting emptiness about Salisbury Plain in southwest England. There are prehistoric burial grounds here, earthworks, camps and stone circles, all showing evidence of early settlements. Yet since then, no villages have grown up and there have been no real signs of life. The undulating chalk plain is 20 miles (32 kilometres) long and about 500 feet (152 metres) above sea level. In 1897 the government began to buy up the land for military use; what remains is planted principally with crops.

ADAM WOOLFITT

rough highlands predominate, and this accentuates the chief ethnic division of the population, between the Anglo-Saxon, deriving from Teutonic invaders who arrived in the Christian era, and the Celtic, descended from far earlier waves of Mediterranean immigration. It was here that the Roman Empire reached its final frontier. The legions never controlled northern Scotland, and they never crossed the Irish Sea. The archipelago was an extremity of the Roman world then, and it remains an extremity of Europe still, never quite assimilated into the European consciousness.

Several of Europe's great historical trends, nevertheless, are epitomized in the British Isles. The continent's ancient dynastic fervours survive here in a rich and ostentatious monarchy. The feudalism that once dominated Europe finds its mementos still in the

obtrusive class system of England and in the kilts, tartans and rituals of the Scottish clans. The religious struggles of the continent, mostly ended elsewhere, survive here in a violent, apparently insoluble and almost stylized conflict between Catholics and Protestants in Northern Ireland. Europe's instinct for aggression and expansion has found some of its most vigorous exponents among these islanders – from the sixteenth century to the twentieth the British were engaged in a career of overseas acquisition which made them briefly the most powerful people on earth, ruling territories in every continent and brazenly commanding all the oceans.

Above all, it was here that Europe first mechanized itself, when the power of steam was harnessed by British scientists and engineers at the end of the eighteenth century.

Oxfordshire, England, United Kingdom

Near Witney, Oxfordshire, a tributary of the Windrush meanders through a stand of fresh-leafed poplars, interrupting their perfectly ordered lines. In the field at left a tractor driver has been equally concerned with the symmetry of his work.

The mastery of technique not only made the British wealthy, but it made them primarily an urban nation – the first in Europe. Today England in particular is one-of the most crowded of all countries, and the vast city of London, sprawled in the southeast corner of the islands in a welter of suburbs and problems, is like an allegory of urban life.

The British attitude to Europe remains ambivalent. No other European Power is an island State, and none has looked so instinctively to the sea for its fortunes. For centuries the British tried to stay clear of continental involvements, intervening only when it seemed that one European Power or another was becoming dangerously dominant. Now their Empire has gone, and their industrial capacity has long been overtaken, but their overseas

Oxford, England, United Kingdom

Gothic spires rise above the halls and quads of Oxford University's 30 colleges. The Radcliffe Camera, the country's first circular library, built in 1748, is to the left of the steeple of St Mary's Church. Below it is the lantern-topped semicircle of Sir Christopher Wren's Sheldonian Theatre.

investments are still enormous, and many older citizens still feel that they have more in common with the other English-speaking peoples, scattered across the world, than with their continental neighbours.

In 1990 the British Isles were for the first time linked by a tunnel to France – a portent, most Europeans thought, of their inevitable absorption into a pan-European system. Old-school Britons, though, remembered with nostalgia a much-loved, frequently quoted but actually apocryphal headline from *The Times* of London:

VIOLENT STORMS IN THE ENGLISH CHANNEL

CONTINENT ISOLATED

London, England, United Kingdom

This is the historical gateway into London: up the Thames estuary and round the great meanders of what was once a bustling dockland. On the near side of Tower Bridge is the Pool of London, the farthest that large ships can navigate. On the left is a glimpse of the Tower of London, the royal residence from the eleventh to the sixteenth centuries. Many of the docks have been filled in as the city's business community has moved eastwards. A skyscraper with a black pyramid roof marks the largest development at Canary Wharf.

ADAM WOOLFITT

112

GEORG RIHA

Trafalgar Square, London, United Kingdom

Diminutive in life, Admiral Horatio Nelson grew enormously in stature on his death in 1805 when he defeated Napoléon's navy at the Battle of Trafalgar, off the southwest coast of Spain. He stands 164 feet (50 metres) above Trafalgar Square, which was laid out in the 1830s on the site of the royal stables. The column was completed in 1842, three years after William Wilkins had finalized the National Gallery, on which Nelson has turned his back. He keeps a watch on Whitehall, the seat of government and power.

The Old Bailey, London, United Kingdom (above)

This is Justice, a nineteenth-century golden figure sculpted by F.W. Pomeroy, with a sword in her right hand and scales to weigh the evidence in her left. She stands above London's Central Criminal Court, usually called the Old Bailey, after the street it faces. This is where some of the country's most unpleasant criminals are brought, and in No. 1 Court, until the abolition of the death penalty in 1965, this is where convicted murderers were sentenced to be hanged.

St Paul's Cathedral, London, United Kingdom (right)

Sir Christopher Wren could only imagine this view of his greatest work. St Paul's Cathedral is London's fifth church on Ludgate Hill. A mixture of Baroque and Classical, it was completed after 36 years in 1710 and was the first purpose-built Protestant cathedral. Its cruciform shape is laid out beneath the 365-foot (110-metre) stone cupola, lantern, ball and cross, around which external galleries provide an elevated view of the city. A Latin inscription on Wren's burial place in the crypt says: 'Reader, if you seek his monument, look around you.'

ADAM WOOLFITT

Ironbridge, Shropshire, England, United Kingdom (left)

It is hard to think of this sparkling gorge on the River Severn in Shropshire as the birthplace of the Industrial Revolution. But near here in 1709 Abraham Darby first smelted iron using coke as a fuel. Seventy years later his grandson designed this bridge, the first in the world to be made of cast iron.

Brighton's Palace Pier, England, United Kingdom (right)

Britain's traditional seasides, of bracing promenades and family fun, are evoked by their piers, and the best-known is Brighton's Palace Pier, defying the waves 1640 feet (500 metres) out to sea. In 1823 the country's first, Chain Pier, was built here, and it served as a jetty for a ferry crossing to Dieppe in France. After a storm brought it down in 1896, the Palace Pier was built to replace it.

Stonehenge, Salisbury Plain, England, United Kingdom (previous pages)

Dawn breaks on Stonehenge and it awakes, stretching its long, lazy shadows eastwards across Salisbury Plain, as it has been doing for about 4000 years. Nobody knows why the massive stones, weighing up to 50 tons (51 tonnes), were brought from Wales; or why they were erected in two concentric circles with a horseshoe shape within.

120

Bradford, Yorkshire, England, United Kingdom (below)

This is a suburb to provoke identity crises: redbrick rows, slate-roofed and serried, with the occasional attic dormer window struggling for a view above the rest. There is nothing to suggest that this is Bradford, Yorkshire's wool and textile city of dark satanic mills. Nor, in these unpeopled side streets, is there anything to convey the city's large Asian population, or the achievements of its inspired sons, such as the artist David Hockney.

ADAM WOOLFITT

ADAM WOOLFITT

Blenheim Palace, Oxfordshire, England, United Kingdom (above)

A grateful country gave part of the Oxfordshire countryside to John Churchill, Duke of Marl-borough, for his military successes in the War of the Spanish Succession, notably at Blenheim in Bavaria, after which this estate was named. The building was designed by Sir John Vanburgh in 1705 and is set in landscaped grounds. In 1874 one of the family home's 200 rooms echoed to the first cries of the infant Winston Churchill.

Llangynog Valley, Wales, United Kingdom (overleaf)

Llangynog Valley is in the heart of north Wales, between the English border and Snowdonia National Park. The language of the people is more often Welsh than English. Trapped in the valley, where the sun's shadow moves like the ebb and flow of the tide, are the small fields of the farmers. But there is no sign of the ponies that are bred for people to trot over the hills for their holidays.

Caernarfon Castle, Wales, United Kingdom (previous pages)

Apart from the cars and the yachts, Caernarfon Castle, on the north coast of Wales, looks much as it must have done when it was built by Edward I following England's conquest of the principality in 1282. Edward's heir was crowned Prince of Wales in the castle, a practice continued right up until today: Prince Charles was invested with the title in a ceremony here in 1969.

PATRICIA AND ANGUS MACDONALD

Loch Eck, Scotland, United Kingdom (below)

This is the essential Scotland of uncompromising mountains, deep narrow lochs, and roads that wind through sparsely inhabited glens. Loch Eck, 6 miles (10 kilometres) long, lies to the southwest of the kingdom. On the left is Glenbranter Forest, on the right Beinn Mhór, high points of the 60000-acre (24280-hectare) Argyll Forest Park. In the glen below, the road leads to the Younger Botanic Garden at Benmore, part of Edinburgh's Royal Botanical Garden.

ADAM WOOLFITT

Edinburgh, Scotland, United Kingdom (above)

The afternoon sun is too weak to melt Edinburgh's snow. On the rock is the city's first building, its castle. The hill slopes down to the right along the Royal Mile and into the medieval old town. Princes Street cuts the scene in half horizontally, dividing the straggling old town from New Town's neat Georgian crescents and squares.

129

Trinity College, Dublin, Republic of Ireland

The great quadrangles of Trinity College, Dublin, focus on a 100-foot (30-metre) campanile erected in 1853 on the site of the medieval monastery church the college replaced when it was built in 1591. Among the treasures in its library is the beautiful late-eighth-century illuminated manuscript, the *Book of Kells*. Beyond the university is the curved façade of the Bank of Ireland, begun in 1729 to house the parliament. O'Connell Bridge leads across the River Liffey to the city's north side.

County Sligo, Republic of Ireland (right)

This great velvet pincushion is 'bare Ben Bulben's head', a 1730-foot (527-metre) mountain between Sligo and Donegal Bay. This part of Ireland is the haunt of the Nobel poet laureate W.B. Yeats (1865–1939) and his artist brother, Jack. Though the poet died in the south of France, his body was returned here to the churchyard at the foot of Ben Bulben.

130

GEORG GERSTER

Kilmacduagh, County Galway, Republic of Ireland (right)

Worn to the colour of the dry bones in the grave-yard that surrounds it, the ruins of the monastery at Kilmacduagh near Gort, County Galway, seem entombed by time. These are some of the remains of the ecclesiastical see founded by St Colman Macduagh in the seventh century. Still standing is a 112-foot (34-metre) tower, leaning 25 inches (64 centimetres) out of perpendicular.

Inishmaan, Aran islands, Republic of Ireland (above)

On the west coast of Ireland, forming a natural breakwater across Galway Bay, are the three Aran islands. This is Inishmaan, between Inisheer and Inishmore. These 'ancient islands of the saints' are peopled by Gaelic-speaking fishermen and farmers. Inishmaan has also attracted such creative talents as John Millington Synge, who was inspired here to write *The Playboy of the Western World*.

132

THE NORTHERNERS

SWEDEN NORWAY DENMARK FINLAND ICELAND

Together with Denmark, the Nordic countries of Norway, Sweden, Finland, Iceland, the Faeroes and Åland form more than a geographical unit. No other such group of European States constitutes a more organic company – ethnically, historically, politically, religiously, artistically and even temperamentally. When somebody speaks of a Scandinavian, an instant stereotype is summoned into almost all our minds.

These countries of the north are mostly ungenerous of terrain, mountainous, sparse and forested. Only Denmark and southern Sweden offer rich pasture land, and Scandinavians have traditionally been obliged to earn their livings in tough vocations, as fishermen, seamen, lumbermen or graziers. Coupled with a paucity of winter sunshine, or even daylight, this has made for those characteristics of strength, taciturnity, introspection and sudden exuberance that the whole world recognizes. Nobody knows the

---

Kronborg Castle, Denmark (left)

This is where Shakespeare set the opening scene of his great tragedy, *Hamlet*, in the port which in Danish is called Helsingør. The castle is Kronborg, and it was completed a dozen years or so before Shakespeare wrote his play.

Jostedalsbreen glacier, Norway (previous pages)

Jostedalsbreen in western Norway is mainland Europe's largest snowfield, covering about 340 square miles (880 square kilometres). The ice can be up to 1650 feet (500 metres) deep, though it is gradually retreating.

origins of the Sami, or Lapps, who live in the extreme north of Sweden, Finland and Norway, sometimes nomadically with reindeers. The Finns evidently originated somewhere in the east. The others, however, are quintessentially Nordic. Except again for the Finns, whose language is akin to Hungarian, they all speak a variety of the same Germanic language. At one time or another most of them have occupied each others' territories or have formed part of the same State — even Iceland was constitutionally subject to Denmark until 1944 — and this has given them, willy-nilly, similar styles of government. The Scandinavian countries (Norway, Sweden and Denmark) have monarchies of the most self-effacing kind, their kings and queens generally preferring populist activities to great parades, and all the Nordic States are governed by staunchly democratic systems. Iceland claims to have the oldest elected assembly on earth, the Altiing having been in existence, except for a hiatus in the nineteenth century, for more than a thousand years.

A streak of the heroic runs through these societies. This was the homeland of the Vikings, the bravos of medieval Europe, whose trading settlements extended as far as the eastern Mediterranean, who reconnoitred Greenland and North America, and whose occupation of Normandy (Norseman's land) led in the end to the conquest of England. The characteristics of a fighting aristocracy are muffled in Scandinavia now, but are remembered always through the great works of medieval literature, the Icelandic Sagas, which record the high-flown pugnacity of the Norwegian kings dwelling in Iceland, and the exploits of legendary heroes.

In modern times the States have been among the least aggressive of all the European countries, devoting themselves chiefly to social progress and enrichment. They were relatively unharmed by the great twentieth-century wars, and they have been famous pioneers of public welfare and successful economic specialists: the Danes as agriculturists, the Norwegians as shipowners, the Swedes as manufacturers of cars, aircraft and machinery, the Finns as lumbermen and shipbuilders. And in the European context they have chiefly been successful, perhaps, in cooperating among themselves. Long before Europe began its present movement towards unity, the Scandinavian countries had established common institutions of their own and had managed to present themselves to the world as a bloc — the first to prove, despite all the historical evidence, that Europeans need not be endemically at each others' throats.

Reykjavík, Iceland

What looks like a puff of smoke to the right of the picture is in fact escaped steam, for Reykjavík is officially a smokeless city, and all its heating is provided by nearby hot springs. Demand is not excessive. Although just on the edge of the Arctic Circle, Iceland has milder winters than New York.

YANN ARTHUS-BERTRAND/ALTITUDE

Dyrehaven, Denmark (above)

A deer herd basks in the sun at Dyrehaven, north of
Copenhagen. This large park is popular for walkers,
cyclists, horse riders and mushroom gatherers.
Adjoining it is a 2500-acre (1000-hectare) beech
wood, where a royal hunting lodge, the Ermitage,
still functions. On the eastern side of the island of
Zealand, there are views from here out across the
Øresund to Sweden. On the south side of the park
is a popular fairground at Bakken.

Frederiksborg Castle, Denmark (right)

The skyline of Frederiksborg Castle is thoroughly
pricked by the gleaming, spiked-helmet roof of
its Gatehouse Tower and other well-honed
architectural points. Built on three islands on a
small lake near Hillerød on Zealand in the
beginning of the seventeenth century, the castle is
seen as the pinnacle of Denmark's Renaissance.
Although named after King Frederick II, who built
an earlier castle here, it was his son, Christian IV,
who was responsible for its present size and shape.
It now houses a Museum of National History.

Broendby, Copenhagen, Denmark (previous pages)

These are the sort of circles many Danes want to move in. Surrounded by sea, the people of Copenhagen like to go inland, to appreciate the flat, fertile island of Zealand. Allotment gardens are a common sight in all of Scandinavia, and here in the suburb of Broendby, just south of the capital, people can find a slice of country life. Planned with great formality, each garden is 4375 square feet (400 square metres), and each chalet is planned to be 440 square feet (40 square metres). In all there are 500 gardens.

YANN ARTHUS-BERTRAND/ALTITUDE

YANN ARTHUS-BERTRAND/ALTITUDE

Copenhagen, Denmark

There is a pleasant openness about the Amalienborg Palace in Copenhagen, with its generous octagonal square approached from four sides. The palace's four wings were originally separate noble houses. Two wings are now occupied by Queen Margrethe II and her family, another by Queen Ingrid the Queen Mother.

Tåsinge, Denmark

Surrounded by its own roofing material, this simple thatched cottage is on
the island of Tåsinge to the south of Fyn, Denmark's third largest island.
This is a romantic countryside. Buried in a nearby cemetery are Count
Sparre, the Swedish nobleman, and Elvira Madigan, a tightrope walker,
whose tragic love story from the last century was made into a film in 1967.

Ålesund, Norway

Ålesund is a town that spills out across the sea, occupying three of the islands or skerries which are liberally scattered all along Norway's western coast. Although an ancient town and one of the country's main fishing ports, none of the old wooden architecture remains. This was replaced by stone buildings after a catastrophic fire in 1904. Thus the church, seen on the middle island of Aspøya, dates from 1909, and many houses are enriched with touches of Art Nouveau.

Skeidharársandur, Iceland (overleaf)

This remote, chilly spot is Skeidharársandur in southern Iceland. Boulders and debris have been brought here by a concentration of glacial flows originating in Iceland's largest glacier. Underground thermal and volcanic activity make the region unpredictable and uninhabitable, and the lack of foxes and other animals make it a safe breeding ground for gulls. Until a bridge was built here in 1976, drivers taking the coastal road had to make a 155-mile (250-kilometre) detour around the region to continue 30 miles (50 kilometres) further along the coast.

ODDBJØRN MONSEN

146

Lake Saimaa, Finland (right)

Timber, pulp, cardboard, paper . . .
these are the exports that keep Finland
afloat. About one-tenth of the country
is covered by its 60000 lakes; most of
the rest is covered by coniferous trees.
The felled logs are transported many
miles through a network of rivers and
lakes. Lake Saimaa covers 500 square
miles (1300 square kilometres) and is the
most southerly part of the system.

Hamina, Finland (above)

Hamina, a port in southern Finland 27 miles (43 kilometres) from the Soviet
border, is built around an octagonal open space planned in 1723. At its hub
is the town hall (1798), to the right is the Orthodox Church of St Peter and
St Paul, and beyond is the white Lutheran church. More than 90 percent of
Finnish people is Lutheran; 1.1 percent is Greek Orthodox.

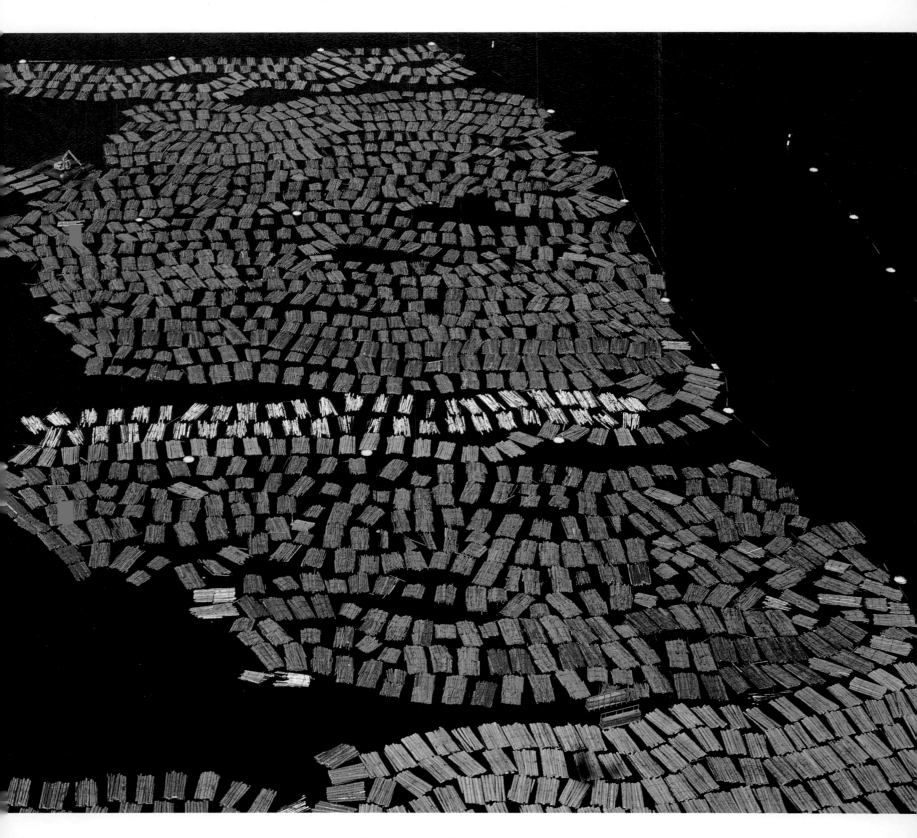

Stockholm, Sweden (overleaf)

Sweden's capital is splashed across a number of islands afloat on the waters that drain into the Baltic Sea. Stockholm's old town is focused on the island of Staden. The Royal Palace occupies the near right-hand corner, royal weddings and coronations take place in the cathedral just behind, and to their right, on its own island, is the parliament building. Opposite the palace is the National Museum.

151

Växjö, Sweden (right)

Typical domestic architecture around Växjö, the county town of Kronoberg, southern Sweden. The woodlands provide much of the region's industry – manufacturing furniture, paper and matches. But this area is also known as the 'Kingdom of Glass' because of its seventeen major glassworks. The techniques were introduced to the country by Gustavus I, who brought the idea from Bohemia.

TORBJORN ANDERSSON

THOMAS STEPHAN

Öland Bridge, Sweden (above)

The Öland Bridge in Sweden takes traffic up and over the Kalmarsund from the mainland town of Kalmar and delivers it to Möllstorp on the island of Öland in the Baltic Sea. Built in 1972 this is Europe's longest bridge, more than 3 miles (6 kilometres) from shore to shore, with 153 piers. It has increased the popularity of this long, narrow and rather flat island as a holiday resort. Among its attractions are Viking rune stones, forts and nearly 400 windmills.

Lake Mälaren, Sweden (overleaf)

This golden corner of the earth is Lake Mälaren, and its beauty makes the facts about it seem hum-drum and dry. Nevertheless they should be stated this is Sweden's third largest lake, covering 440 square miles (1140 square kilometres) and stocked with 1200 islands totalling 189 square miles (490 square kilometres). Its surface water is about 12 inches (30 centimetres) above sea level, and until the Middle Ages it was a marine bay. It lies inland from Stockholm, to which it is connected by canals.

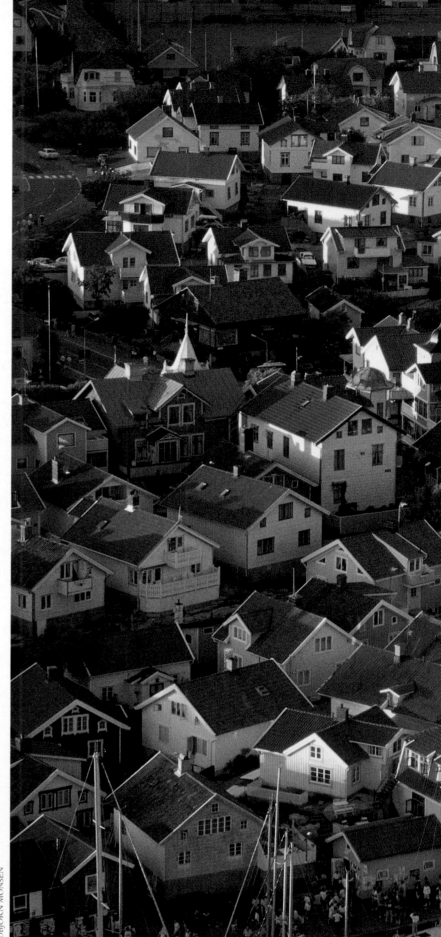

THOMAS STEPHAN

ODDBJØRN MONSEN

Uppsala, Sweden

Uppsala's tidy, symmetrical cathedral is Sweden's largest church and its towers rise 390 feet (119 metres). It was consecrated in 1435 and given its northern Gothic look by a French architect, Etienne de Bonneuil. Gustavus I (1496–1560), founder of modern Sweden, is buried here, and so is Linnaeus (1707–78), founder of modern botany. The old university town of Uppsala is also the see of the Lutheran Archbishop of Sweden.

Smögen, Sweden

The white houses of Smögen give the island a clean and healthy holiday air. Along the quayside tourists browse in the shops and admire the boats in one of Sweden's most popular sailing resorts. The fishing is good here, too, and shrimp are a particular favourite. Smögen is north of Gothenburg and is connected to the mainland by a 1320-foot (403-metre) bridge.

Gothenburg, Sweden (right)

The red-and-white 'Utkiken' ('lookout') building, owned by the Skanska construction company, stand like a lighthouse beside the Göta River in Sweden's second-largest city. Below it is a gleaming shopping centr the Lilla Bommen harbour for visiting small craft, and the *Viking*, a tall ship where sea cooks and technicians are trained. Gothenburg is Scandinavia's largest port, and when it was founded in the seventeenth century many Dutch came here and laid out its canals.

Gamla Uppsala, Sweden (above)

These three man-made hillocks may be the last resting place of kings Adil, Egil and Aun. They are the largest of a group of burial mounds in Gamla (Old) Uppsala, just north of Uppsala and the ancient home of Sweden's kings. Dating from about 500 AD, the *Folkvandringstiden* or 'time of migration' which preceded the Viking era, the mounds lie along a natural ridge beside the parish church built on Scandinavia's last pagan temple.

160

THE LOW COUNTRIES

THE NETHERLANDS
BELGIUM LUXEMBOURG

O n the map the Low Countries look as though they are a single State, and once they were. They are the flatlands that surround the North Sea estuaries of three rivers, the Rhine, the Meuse and the Scheldt. At the end of the nineteenth-century Napoleonic wars, after a complex history of dynastic exchange and rivalry, they were briefly united as the Kingdom of the Low Countries; but in the old way of Europe the comity did not last, and they are now divided once more into the kingdoms of Belgium and the Netherlands, and the Grand Duchy of Luxembourg.

They have much in common. They are all small countries – Luxembourg indeed, with an area less than 1000 square miles (about 2600 square kilometres), is the smallest truly independent, sovereign State in Europe. Their histories have often coincided. Their countrysides are mostly uniformly flat. Their peoples are all Germanic in origin, and long

---

Delft, Netherlands (left)

In the sixteenth and seventeenth centuries, Delft flourished as a centre of Catholic humanism and the arts. One famous son was Hugo Grotius (1583–1645), an early advocate of international law, whose statue is partially hidden by the spire of the New Church.

Texel Island, Netherlands (previous pages)

The island of Texel in north Holland is a flat pancake, with its rim turned up to keep out the tides. On the northern side a long beach is backed by dunes; on the near side a dike holds back the Waddenzee.

Loosdrechtse Plassen, Netherlands

The Dutch are immensely imaginative in their use of water and waterways. They have had to be, for theirs is the most densely populated corner of Europe, and a quarter of their country lies below sea level. This is part of the Loosdrechtse Plassen, an area of seven lakes between Amsterdam and Utrecht, where over the years the dikes have eroded.

THOMAS STEPHAN

before the European Common Market came into being they had established their own customs union. Their reputations and destinies, though, have been very different.

Pre-eminent among the three is the Netherlands, more accurately but less officially known as Holland, which has a population of less than 16 million, but has been one of Europe's pace-makers and power-houses. Great sailors, merchants, engineers, patrons and practitioners of art, the Dutch literally created their own country, for a quarter of it has been reclaimed from the sea, and it is now the most densely populated State in Europe. From this precarious seashore base, as vulnerable to the elements as it was to enemies from the European interior, the Dutch sailed out to seize for themselves one of the biggest of the overseas Empires. Even now the Dutch flag flies over several islands of the Caribbean, and the language of the South African Afrikaners is a kind of Dutch. With the spoils of the east they made themselves rich, and they have remained rich by astute trading, by innovative industry, and by exploiting the geographical advantage of their position at the mouth of the Rhine. Huge industries have grown up around the port of Rotterdam – chief outlet to the sea for Germany, and one of the world's busiest seaports – and some of the great Dutch companies are worldwide in their presence.

No such vivid images attach themselves to Belgium, the butt of many jokes from Europeans of more flamboyant background. Belgium is indeed an unassertive country, and well it might be, for nowhere in Europe has been more cruelly ravaged by the comings and goings of foreign armies. Waterloo is in Belgium, and so is Ypres, and here are the forests of the Ardennes where Hitler's armies made their last counterattack in the west.

Antwerp, Belgium

Antwerp, the fifth-largest port in the world, lies on the River Schelde in Belgium, 55 miles (88 kilometres) from the North Sea. It was the home of Peter Paul Rubens (1577–1640) whose masterpiece, a triptych called *Descent from the Cross*, is housed in the Gothic Cathedral of Our Lady.

This is Europe's cockpit. A nation-State since only 1831, when it was separated from the Netherlands, Belgium is inhabited partly by Flemings of Latin origin, who speak a form of Dutch, and partly by Walloons of Celtic origin, who speak French. Thickly populated, heavily industrialized, producing few things that most of us know about, boasting few heroes that we have heard of, Belgium came paradoxically but justly out of its obscurity when its capital Brussels became the administrative headquarters of the European Community and thus became a synonym for bureaucracy.

And what of Luxembourg? Oddly enough, for many decades it was a prime symbol of Europeanism. The Grand Duchy was once very much grander, including the whole of what is now Belgium, and it has remained a formidable little State. Its steel production is said to be the highest per capita in the world; it is an eager centre of international finance and the legal capital of the European Community. However, what made it seem long ago a supra-European State was the presence there of an international commercial broadcasting industry, transmitting in many languages. In the days when a united Europe seemed no more than a pipedream, the familiar name of Radio Luxembourg carried to listeners far away a first faint inkling of community.

Lisse, Netherlands

Ribbed like corduroy, these Dutch bulb fields near Lisse become bright coloured stripes in April and May as tulips come into bloom. Flowers are picked in the evening and auctioned next morning. At Aalsmeer, between Lisse and Amsterdam, 11 million flowers and 1 million plants are sold every day. Nearby, close to Schiphol airport, there are two further auction houses, and flowers can be air-freighted and on sale in most major world cities within 24 hours.

THOMAS STEPHAN

MAX DERETA

MAX DERETA

Rotterdam, Netherlands (above)

This is the world's largest and busiest port. Rotterdam is 19 miles (30 kilometres) upriver from the North Sea and Europoort, where most petroleum companies have refining facilities. Through the city runs the Nieuwe Maas, spanned here by the red Willems Bridge. Its waterways connect with the Rhine and lead into the heart of industrial Germany. Heavy bombing in the Second World War has meant the city is largely of modern design, though a very small part of the old port remains, in the top left of the picture.

Gelderland, Netherlands (right)

St Hubert's Hunting Lodge was designed to look like a deer's antlers. It was built for Helene Kröller-Müller, the wife of a shipping magnate, between 1915 and 1920. The lodge was in their 22-square-mile (57-square-kilometre) estate, now De Hoge Veluwe National Park in Gelderland in the middle of Holland. While here Mrs Kröller-Müller built up one of the country's finest art collections, still housed in the Kröller-Müller Museum, which she also had built on the estate.

Amsterdam, Netherlands (previous pages)

Amsterdam, capital of the Netherlands, takes its name from the
River Amstel, its principal canal. Red-and-white tourist boats are
moored on it, in the middle of the picture; at the top right it
passes the twentieth-century town hall and opera house; and the
wide street to the left of the canal is Rokin Street.

174

Scheveningen, Netherlands

The Hague is home to the Dutch parliament and the International Courts of Justice. Just a short tram ride away is Scheveningen on the North Sea. A fashionable resort since the nineteenth century, it has a pier, wide sandy beaches, and the Kurhaus, a hotel with restaurants, bars and casino, which dominates the sea front.

175

O V E R   E U R O P E

Esch-sur-Sûre, Luxembourg

A meander in the twinkling River Sûre forms an almost-complete moat around the medieval castle of Esch-sur-Sûre in Luxembourg. At night the ruins of a tenth-century fort and a church in front of it are floodlit, making it one of the Grand Duchy's special attractions. The town is in the north of the small country in the forest of the Ardennes.

THOMAS STEPHAN

DANIEL PHILIPPE

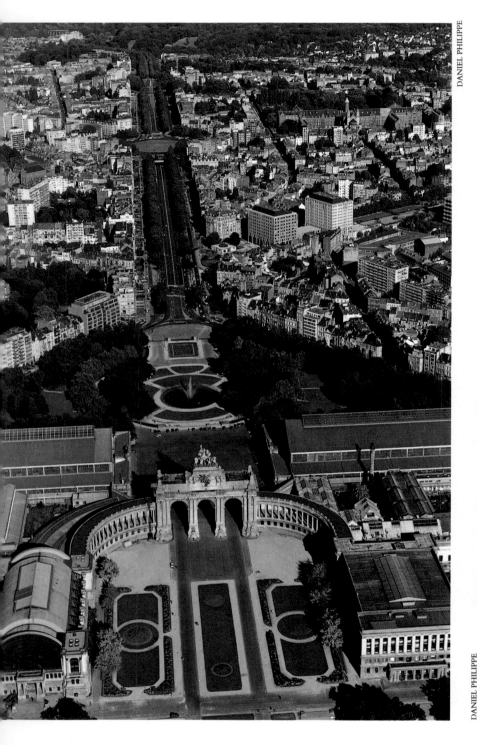

DANIEL PHILIPPE

Brussels, Belgium (above)

Belgium's capital, Brussels, is often thought of as the capital of the whole continent of Europe, perhaps because both the European Commission and NATO have their headquarters here. Its earlier glory is reflected in this huge archway, the Cinquantenaire. Attached to it are an aviation museum (bottom left) and the Royal Museums of Art and History (bottom right).

Waterloo, Belgium (above)

On this Belgian field on 18 June 1815, modern Europe's most ambitious and talented general was finally defeated. At Waterloo Napoléon Bonaparte, emperor of France, was trounced in a two-day battle by allied forces under Britain's Duke of Wellington and Prussia's von Blücher. This commemorative statue of a lion marks the spot where the 23-year-old Prince of Orange, son of William I of the Netherlands, was wounded in the shoulder.

THE HEARTLANDS

GERMANY AUSTRIA SWITZERLAND

I n the very heart of Europe, at the centre of its preoccupations for hundreds of years, lies a language – German – the language of Goethe and Schiller and Beethoven and Martin Luther, of Einstein and Benz, of Adolf Hitler. The energies of this powerful tongue, which inspires a particular loyalty among all who use it, have frequently governed the course of history and bind these territories together not only linguistically but also in style and often in emotion.

It is true that in one of the States of this Germanic core, Switzerland, three other national languages are officially recognized as well – French, Italian and Romansh – but then Switzerland, which is not even a member of the United Nations, stands outside every norm, in its wealth, beauty, complacency and conservatism, as in its constitutional neutrality. Austria too is *sui generis* as a State, being the rump of the once-mighty Habsburg

---

Cologne, Germany (left)

Cologne Cathedral appears like a haunting spirit from a Gothic tale, out of place with the modern, post-Second World War city around it. This is what aerial bombing did; suddenly gone forever were so many monuments, so many tangible links with the past.

Reinharz Castle, Germany (previous pages)

In the muted early-morning light of an east German spring, trees not yet fully in leaf are silhouetted in the pale waters of a small lake belonging to Reinharz Castle. Set among farmlands to the north of Halle, the Baroque 'water castle' was built in 1701.

This is where Switzerland, Europe's most mountainous country, began. On the lefthand side of the large promontory that protrudes into Lake Uri is a lakeside terrace under the cliffs. Here is a meadow called Rütli, where in 1307 the people of three cantons, Uri, Schwyz and Unterwalden, met and swore an Everlasting League to free themselves of their Hapsburg rulers and start the unique independent confederation of communities. Opposite the tip of the promontory is the picturesque small town of Brunnen.

Empire. And Liechtenstein is only just a State, for its foreign affairs, its defence, its postal services and even its currencies are managed by the Swiss.

But Germany itself, the cradle of the language, exerts such powerful suggestions and has played so important and sometimes terrible a part in the history of the twentieth century, that its status has become almost a metaphor for the destiny of Europe. When in 1990 its two halves were reunited after thirty years of Cold War alienation, this event more than any other seemed to carry the promise of a Europe reconciled; for without a strong, stable and peaceable Germany at its centre, the idea of Europe loses its potency.

It is a relative newcomer among the nation-States, as it is among the democracies. Split for centuries into fissiparous principalities, disrupted again by the sixteenth-century Reformation which was later to divide all Europe, addled by countless wars and dynastic settlements, it became a modern unified State only in 1871. Even into the twentieth century Prussians, Saxons and Bavarians hardly recognized themselves as of the same

nationality, for all their common heritage of language, and even now Germany remains a federation of disparate provinces.

Many kinds of terrain are to be found in this microcosm of the continent. There are Baltic ports and North Sea beaches; there are the Alps of Bavaria and the forests of Baden-Württemberg; Hamburg, in the northwest, is a famously liberal and outward-looking seaport, with old British connections; Munich, in the southeast, is a paradigm of German continentalism, close to Switzerland, Austria, Italy and Czechoslovakia. The eastern provinces, so long stifled by communism, remain drably behind the times; in the west the cult of materialism is to be seen at its glitziest and most successful.

For the most part the Germanic peoples have concerned themselves with Europe, their excursions into overseas colonialism having been brief and limited. The work of their geniuses has of course become part of the whole world's cultural inheritance, so that Mozart and Freud seem to be compatriots of us all, but their language remains almost symbolically European. And in Germany stands the city that more than any other exemplifies the mixed significance of this continent. Berlin, standing more or less at its epicentre, is because of Adolf Hitler a place of evil memory; but reunited as it is now around the fulcrum of the Brandenburg Gate, with its equivocal emanations of tragedy, merriment, new hope and a lingering distrust, backed by the wealth and power of Germany, it is the natural capital of Europe.

Sans Souci Palace, Potsdam, Germany

Sans Souci Palace in Potsdam, southwest of Berlin, is the pride of old Prussia. The single-storey rococo summer palace was built in 1747 by the architect Georg Wenzeslaus von Knobelsdorff to the plans of Frederick the Great. The gardens are ordered around a former terraced vineyard, and the whole complex of buildings and parklands covers 716 acres (290 hectares). In August 1991, 205 years after his death, Frederick's remains were ceremoniously returned to his home here.

Frankfurt am Main, Germany (overleaf)

The twin black towers of the Deutsche Bank are the flagships of modern Frankfurt, the financial capital of Germany. They look down over the park where the city's medieval fortifications once stood. This was a major settlement under Charlemagne, and the birthplace of the writer Goethe in 1749. The Alte Oper concert hall, on the right, was reconstructed after the Second World War.

GEORG GERSTER

186

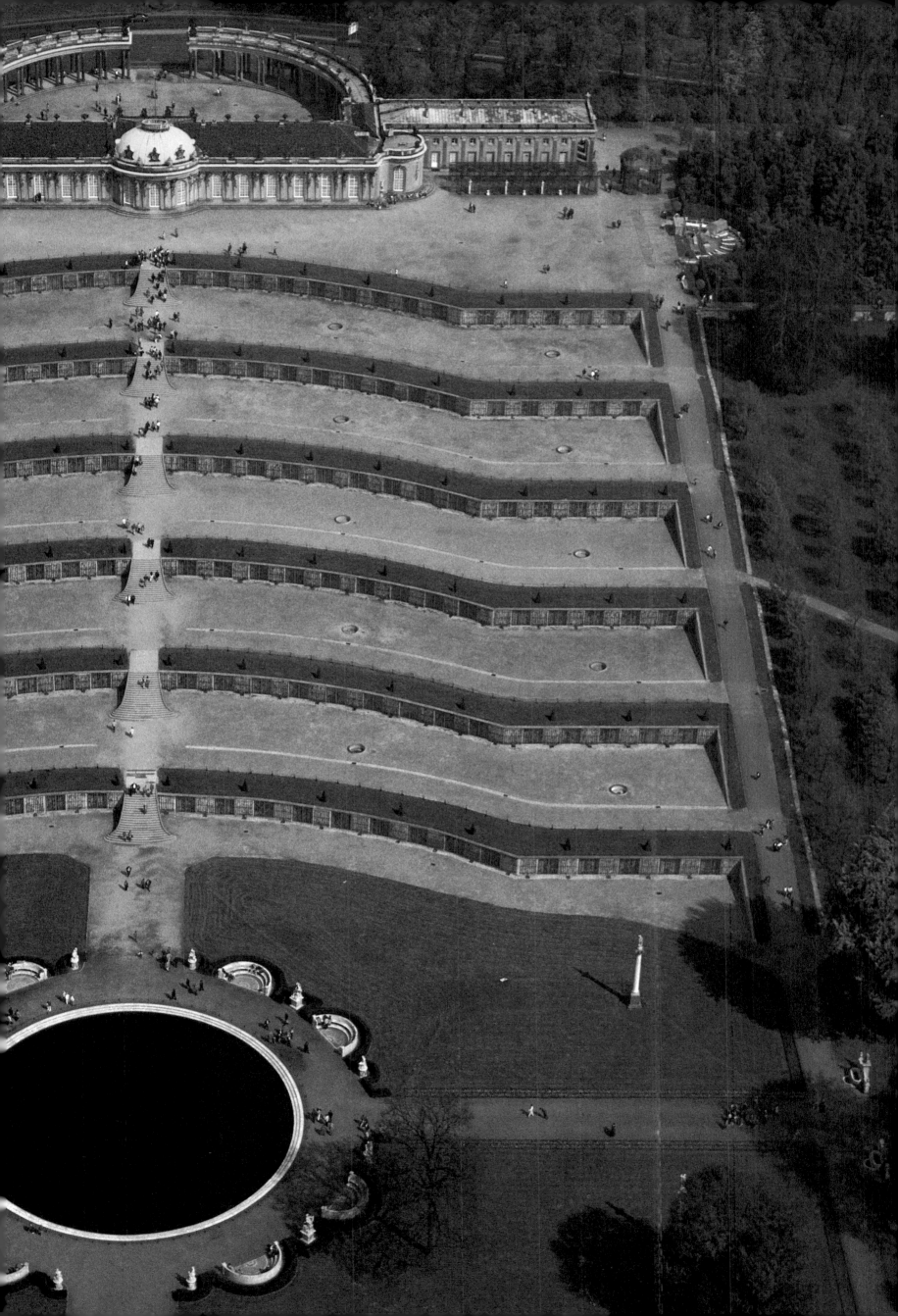

Saxony, Germany (left)

These introverted farm buildings, facing each other across large court-yards, are between Leipzig and Dresden in eastern Germany. This kind of farm is called a Vierseithof. Its half-timbered buildings are easier to manage set around a quadrangle, but one of the original purposes of the design was for protection against attack. Typically these are mixed farms with a few animals and just one large field for crops.

Dresden, Germany (right)

The Hofkirche, or Court Cathedral, in Dresden has turned its back on us. Instead of facing east, it faces southwest so that it can look out across the River Elbe. A Roman Catholic church, it was one of the last Italian Baroque churches to be built in Europe, in the mid-eighteenth century.

Upper Bavaria, Germany (overleaf)

Snow wipes the colour away from a winter scene in Upper Bavaria, south of Munich, reducing it to monochrome. This is Moosrain, part of the village of Gmund on the north shore of the Tegernsee. Holiday-makers come here year-round. In winter there are cross-country ski trails, while nearby mountains provide speedy slopes. In the summer it is hikers' terrain.

The Rhine, Germany

Commercially, the Rhine is Europe's most important waterway. It flows from the Alps through Switzerland, along the Austrian, German and French borders, and through Germany and the Netherlands to the North Sea. In the Middle Rhine, between Mainz and Koblenz, is the pretty fourteenth-century Pfalzgrafenstein (Customs House), still attending its island post.

194

Iller Valley, Bavaria, Germany (overleaf)

The Iller Valley in the Allgäu, Bavaria, is a land of
ponds, moors and meadows, lying beneath mountains
that climb towards Austria. It is a popular tourist region
year-round. Here at Illertal bei Martinszell the summer
landscape takes on the colours and texture of oil paint.
The warm green of the pastureland is cut by a rich,
deep blue made by the River Iller and by the shadows
cast by the firs, while the sunless hollows of the stepped,
chalk terraces become splashes of a brighter blue.

THOMAS STEPHAN

THOMAS STEPHAN

Lübeck, Germany (right)

Lübeck, 'Queen of the Hansa', was the capital of
the Hanseatic League of trading towns which
stretched from the Netherlands to Poland,
monopolizing trade across the Baltic to Russia and
Scandinavia. The brick-built town arose on an
island on the River Trave and could be approached
through the sturdy Holstentor, the twin round-
towered gate in the medieval walls seen on the
bottom left. On the right are the twin towers of St
Mary's, completed in 1330 for the city burghers.

195

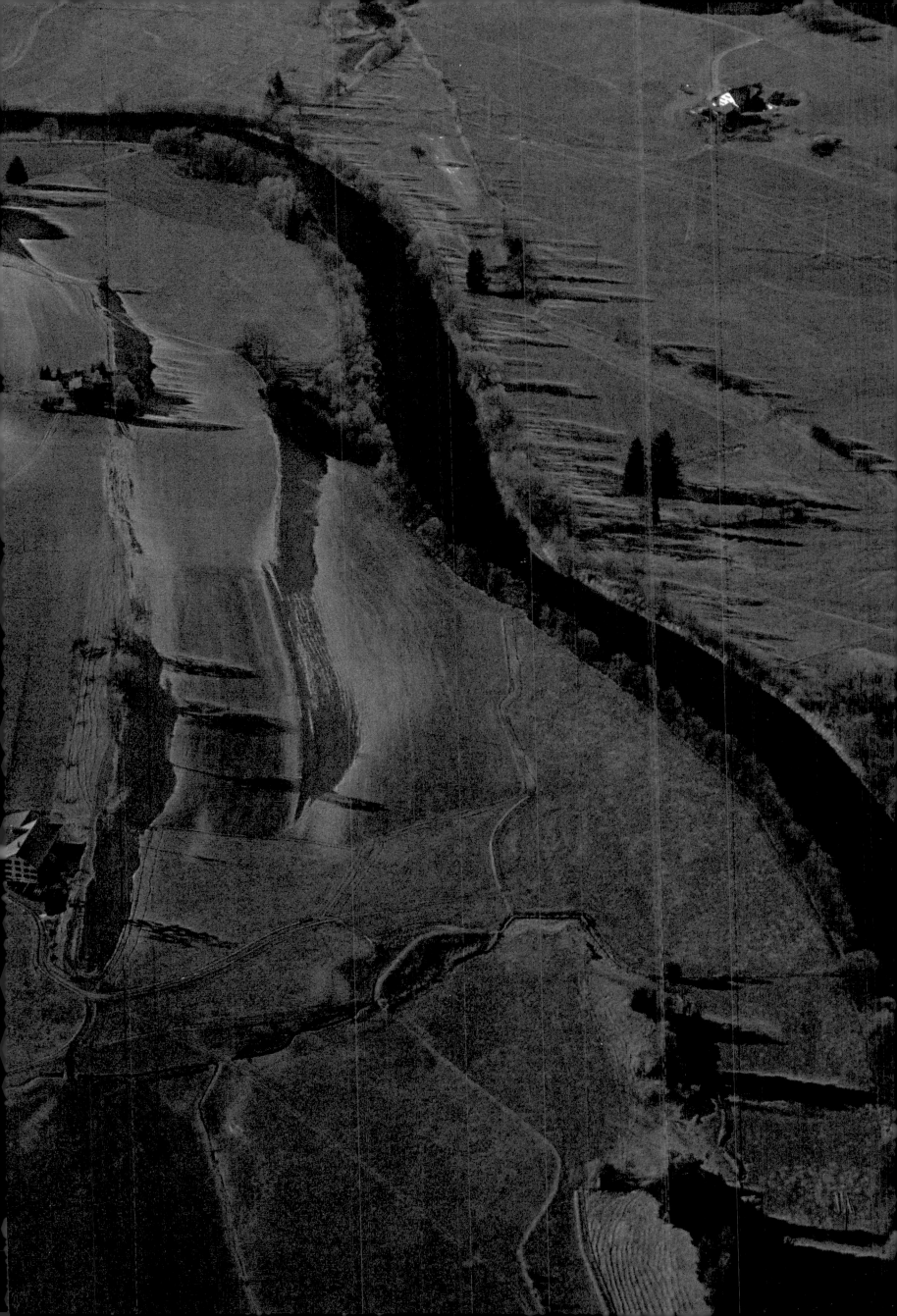

GEORG GERSTER

Museum Island, Berlin, Germany (right)

Afloat between two arms of the Spree are the cathedral and great museums of Berlin. On the near, north side is the domed Bode Museum, and just beyond is the neo-classical Pergamon, which houses some of the most impressive sculpture and architecture from the Classical world. Behind the cathedral on the opposite bank is Marx-Engels-Platz and, in the far corner, the town hall.

Unter den Linden, Berlin, Germany (above)

Unter den Linden (Under the Lime Trees) is the best-known street in Berlin. It was laid out in the seventeenth century with 1000 lime trees and 1000 nut trees. In the middle is a statue of Prussia's Frederick the Great, born here in 1712. At the far end lies the Brandenburg Gate, once the symbol of a Germany divided between East and West.

Town Hall, Munich, Germany (right)

Marienplatz is the heart of the Bavarian capital of Munich. Here is where people meet, to sit out at the cafe tables or inside the beer halls. Rising beside them on a small plinth is a gold statue of the Virgin Mary (erected in 1638), after whom the square is named. The ornate white tower looking down over it belongs to the nineteenth-century town hall. Twice a day its clock chimes, and mechanical figures come out to dance.

THOMAS STEPHAN

THOMAS STEPHAN

English Garden, Munich, Germany (above)

The Englischer Garten in Munich is Europe's largest city park. On summer evenings people bring picnics here to the beer garden at the Chinese pagoda, where they eat and drink at communal trestle tables. The garden was designed in 1790 by the Anglo-American physician and politician Lord Romford.

Offingen, Germany (overleaf)

The village of Offingen in Upper Swabia, south of Stuttgart, pulls a duvet
of hoarfrost around itself as the faint sun of a January dawn tries to prize
it from sleep. Blue with cold, the wooded hillside called Bussen encircles
the church dedicated to Our Lady of Sorrow. This Gothic building was
founded in 1516, and it attracts a number of pilgrims every year.

THOMAS STEPHAN

Leipzig, Germany (right)

This is a legacy of the Third Reich, which looked to mythology to inspire nationalism. The Nibelungen-Ring in Leipzig is a 1930s housing estate constructed in 'mystical' rings around Siegfried Square. The composer Richard Wagner was born in the city in 1813. Lying on the confluence of three rivers 90 miles (145 kilometres) southwest of Berlin, Leipzig has been known as 'the secret capital of east Germany', and Goethe, who set *Faust* in one of its taverns, called it 'little Paris'.

GEORG GERSTER

GEORG GERSTER

Neuschwanstein Castle, Germany (left)

This is where Disneyland began. Neuschwanstein Castle was the greatest indulgence of the. insane castle builder and Wagner patron, King Ludwig II of Bavaria. It was created by the theatre designer Jank von Dollmann and built between 1886 and 1889. High on a rock, it overlooks the Allgäu mountains near the Austrian border. Each year 1.5 million people visit the castle, which was copied for the centrepiece of Disneyland in America.

Halle, Germany (overleaf)

Postwar planning in the German Democratic Republic left the Paulus Church (1903) the focal point of a suburban district of the industrial city of Halle, northwest of Leipzig. The town is first mentioned in a document dating from AD 806, referring to fortifications to be built around saline springs which for many centuries gave the city its wealth. Lying on the Saale, which feeds the Elbe, it was also a river port. The composer George Frederick Handel was born here in 1685.

GEORG RIHA

GEORG RIHA

Schönbrunn Palace, Vienna, Austria (above)

Two grassy hearth rugs have been put down
in the grand courtyard of Schönbrunn Palace in
Vienna. This was the summer residence of the
Habsburgs, bought in 1569. A century later it was
remodelled, and then was given a more modest
aspect. Napoléon stayed here, and this is where
Franz Joseph I (1830–1916) was born and died. In
the palace grounds is the world's oldest zoo.

St Stephen's Cathedral, Vienna, Austria (right)

The diamond-patterned glazed-tile roof of St
Stephen's Cathedral in Vienna, rebuilt since the
Second World War, is so steeply pitched that at
first glance it seems to rise up like a pointed tower.
When the 450-foot (137-metre) south tower,
known as 'Steffl', was put up it was considered
too proud and lofty, and plans for a matching tower
on the north side were cut short. But the lower
tower (far left) provided a firmer base for
'Pummerin' ('Boomer'), Austria's largest bell.

208

Salzburg, Austria

Salzburg, birthplace of
Mozart and one of Europe's
most musical cities, lies
silent in the snow. In the
background is the shadowy
bulk of the Hohensalzburg
fortress, dating mainly from
1500. Below it the sun
catches the seventeenth-
century towers of the west
front of the cathedral.
The angular building on
this side of it, centred on
three large marble
courtyards, is the palace
of the prince-bishops who
ruled from the thirteenth
century. Mozart was born
in a house between here
and the Salzach River.

GEORG RIHA

211

GEORG RIHA

The Road of the Cellars, Austria (above)

'Kellergasse' is the Road of the Cellars, a row
of small farmhouses each sitting on top of cavernous
basements where the produce of the gently rolling
hills around them is kept. The strips of land,
coloured according to their state of cultivation, are
all planted with vines. The loamy ground absorbs
the sun's rays to make the region in Lower Austria,
some 25 miles (40 kilometres) northeast of Vienna,
one of the country's main wine-producing centres.

Eastern Tyrol, Austria (right)

The little church dedicated to St Korbinian sits on a
hillock overlooking the Pustertal valley in Austria's
eastern Tyrol. Its treasures include works by Michael
Pacher, better known for the stunning high altar
he completed in 1482 in the church at St Wolfgang
(now a health resort) in Upper Austria. Along the
Pustertal's broad valley runs the Drau, which
eventually flows into the Danube in Yugoslavia.
On its north side are the Defereggen mountains,
where pretty villages bask on a 'sun terrace'.

212

GEORG RIHA

EMIL SCHULTHESS

Zurich, Switzerland

The spire of St Peter's Church, which has clock faces measuring some 29 feet (9 metres) in diameter, looks out across Zurich, Switzerland's largest city. The camera has distorted the curve in the Limmat River, which runs in to the city from Lake Zurich (off to the right of the picture), past the twin towers of the Grossmünster, to the seventeenth-century Rathaus jutting out into the river on the far bank (near the centre of the picture). The Rathaus is still used by the town and canton parliaments.

215

THE CENTRAL EUROPEANS

POLAND CZECHOSLOVAKIA HUNGARY

Until the end of the Cold War in 1990, the countries we think of as Central Europe – Poland, Czechoslovakia, Hungary – had hardly seemed part of the contemporary continent. They stood beyond the Iron Curtain as if bewitched by the spell of Stalinism, and looked for their economic, cultural and military support not to their old partners in the European tradition, but to the mostly Asiatic Soviet Union, with which they all share frontiers to the east. Yet all three are partners in Europe's Christian heritage and are linked by innumerable strands of history with the nation-States to the west.

In 1938 the Prime Minister of Great Britain, excusing his country's reluctance to go to Czechoslovakia's defence, described it as 'a far-away country that we know little of'. Nevertheless these countries have never been beyond the concerns of Europe, and in particular the concerns of the German-speaking nations, with which all three have

---

Mazury, Poland (left)

Autumn colours the ancient woods of Mazury, northeast Poland, one of Europe's most bountiful natural regions. There are 90 nature reserves, wild buffalo, Europe's largest elk herd, and the world's smallest forest ponies.

Zwierzyniec, Poland (previous pages)

The monastery of Bielany in Zwierzyniec looks a remote refuge, but in fact it is just a bus ride from Kraków. The monks belong to the strict Cameldolite order, established in 1604, which allows them no contact with the outside world.

219

The Mátra, northern Hungary

This is the Mátra, the highlands of northern Hungary, about 55 miles (90 kilometres) northeast of Budapest. In summer the slopes produce excellent wines, particularly around the town of Gyöngyös (a white wine called Debrői Hárslevelű is recommended). From here a narrow-gauge railway goes up to the most popular ski resort of Mátrafüred.

common frontiers to the west. Almost land-locked (only Poland has a sea-coast, on the Baltic), with Russia on one flank, Germany on the other, they have been battlegrounds throughout their histories and have been plagued by all the old European problems of minorities and disputed boundaries.

Ethnically mixed, they are nevertheless among the most strongly nationalistic countries of the continent. The Poles look back to centuries of tragic defiance, as their country has been divided, enlarged or diminished at the will of stronger Powers. Hilaire Belloc once called Poland 'the hope of the half-defeated'. Hungary remembers the days when it was an equal partner in the Austro-Hungarian Empire, and still further back to its own pre-eminence under the Magyar kings of the Middle Ages. Czechoslovakia has been a State only since 1918, when it was created out of the fragmented Habsburg Empire, and is still

divided between the predominantly urbanized Czechs and the chiefly rural Slovaks, but its loyalties are centred on the magnificent and historic city of Prague, one of the most beautiful in all Europe and in itself an exhibition of European civilization.

A range of mountains dominates Czechoslovakia, but Poland and Hungary are mostly flat, allowing the easy entry of armies. Here successive waves of invaders from the east have reached the limits of their expansion – Mongols, Muslims, Soviet Communists – and here before the Second World War lived the world's greatest population of Jews, most of them murdered by fellow-Europeans in the concentration camps of Nazi-occupied Poland.

For the most part the people of these countries have always lived austerely. There is coal in Poland and bauxite in Hungary, but traditionally these have been agricultural lands with a labour force of peasantry. Only in the west of Czechoslovakia, old Bohemia and Moravia, is there an old-established industrial base, and even now, when the whole area has been homogenized by nearly half a century of communism, the gilded cities of the old regimes contrast piquantly with the poor villages of the countrysides. Yet these are States of consequence, strong in their own loyalties, and forming a kind of buffer, extending north and south across much of Europe, between the venerable and elaborate cultures of the west and Asia's ever-threatening influence.

Gdańsk, Poland

The individually styled gables of these colourful five-storey houses look Dutch: some acutely angled, some stepped, and some with the curvacious lines of a cello or violin. But they are not in Holland; they are in Poland in the old town of Gdańsk, showing what links there have been between northern Europe's neighbours for so many hundred years. Trade with Germany and Flanders via the Baltic was active in the ninth century, and the prosperous building boom came in the sixteenth and seventeenth centuries.

Gdańsk, Poland (overleaf)

Shipyards look similar all over the world, but this one in Gdańsk became a symbol. This shipyard was where the trade union Solidarity caught the world's attention as it fought for freedoms under Poland's communist rule. After more than a decade of struggle, its leader, Lech Wałęsa, became the country's president, leaving the yard to get on with the business of making and repairing ships, an industry that has been carried on here for at least 700 years.

GEORG GERSTER

222

Jasna Góra, Częstockowa, Poland (below)

More than 90 percent of Poles are Roman Catholics, and Jasna Góra, northwest of Kraków, is one of their most venerated shrines. Its focal point is a painting of a Black Madonna. Two cuts in her cheek are said to have been made by an angry thief, who found it getting heavier and heavier as he tried to carry it away.

GEORG GERSTER

GEORG GERSTER

Marienburg, Poland (above)

Begun in 1274, the pink castle of Marienburg was a major bastion
of the Teutonic Order of knights. Situated in north Poland, just inland
from Gdańsk, it was a base for the knights' forays into the east as they
helped to carve out the Baltic empire. In 1466 it came under Polish
administration, and today medieval events are re-enacted there.

227

Mazury, Poland (previous pages)

In Mazury, northeast Poland, a tractor systematically
wipes the colour from a field like an eraser. In this
sparsely populated region is a sect of Russian Old
Believers, a community that has lived here since the
seventeenth century, intermarrying and keeping its
archaic language alive.

GEORG GERSTER

GEORG GERSTER

Warsaw, Poland (above)

Lined up in stoic silence, these housing blocks seem to be waiting for
someone to tell them what to do. This is the Bródno quarter of
Warsaw, a middle-class housing district which was built in the 1970s.
Even though the buildings are spread out, the open areas between them
are not enough to prevent some living in the shadows of others.

230

Old Warsaw, Poland (above)

The whimsical tilt of the roofs and the simple house façades make this picture
seem like the work of an Eastern European naive artist. This is Rynek Starego
Miasta, the square at the heart of old Warsaw. It suffered in the systematic
destruction of the city by the Nazis following the 1944 uprising, but immediately
after the war it was reconstructed using photographs, engravings and paintings.

Charles Bridge, Prague, Czechoslovakia

Charles Bridge is Prague's most delightful artery. Traffic is no longer allowed on this 1980-foot (603-metre) bridge, which was designed in the fourteenth century by a 27-year-old architect, Peter Parler of Grund, who supposedly bonded its stones with mortar mixed with eggs. Its 30 statues were added in the eighteenth and nineteenth centuries. From the old town on the near bank of the Vltava, the bridge leads over the river to Malá Strana, the old noble quarter, and the city's castle.

Southern Poland (previous pages)

South of Kraków, the former capital of Poland, chequered farmlands blanket the slopes of the Carpathian mountains. Rising toward the Czechoslovakian border are the Tatra mountains, the highest part of the range, rising to 8625 feet (2655 metres). Summer resorts and winter sports centres bring holiday-makers to the region.

GEORG GERSTER

234

Prague, Czechoslovakia (right)

Prague 2, Vinohrady District was once the best
address for officials and the upper middle class of
Czechoslovakia's capital. 'Vinohrady' means
vineyards, which is what this land just east of the
old town was given over to until the last century.
Ideally located, the garden squares were built to a
modern urban design at the beginning of this
century. But now pollution and a deterioration
in the buildings' fabric has forced its traditional
residents further away.

GEORG GERSTER

GEORG GERSTER

St Nicholas's Church, Prague, Czechoslovakia (left)

St Nicholas's in Old Town Square, Prague, wears
a creamy white, well-starched gown beneath the
worn green ruffs of its roof. There has been a
church on this site since the thirteenth century,
but its present form dates from 1732. In 1883,
in a house just beside it, the writer Franz Kafka
was born. The Baroque age attracted many artists
and craftsmen to the city, paid for by rich and
noble foreigners who settled here.

Hluboká Castle, southern Bohemia, Czechoslovakia (overleaf)

The British royal family may not recognize it, but this is supposed to be a replica of Windsor Castle. Hluboká Castle, founded in the thirteenth century, was rebuilt in the late nineteenth century; and by the time it was confiscated by the government in 1945 it was the centre of the largest private domain in Czechoslovakia. Lying in a park above the Vltava River, it is today open to the public.

Carlsbad, Czechoslovakia

This is where Europe's rich and royal used to come for their curative baths. Karlovy Vary in Bohemia, Czechoslovakia, better known as Carlsbad, grew prosperous on its thermal springs after the main one was discovered in the fourteenth century. Charles IV was said to have been led to it by a deer while out hunting. The spa has twelve springs, which are still in use for cures and treatments, although the scaffolding on some of the buildings hints at the cost of maintaining the resort's rich architectural legacy.

Southern Moravia, Czechoslovakia (above)

For mile upon mile the farmlands of southern Moravia are scratched clean and planted with fruit trees, in particular with apricots and peaches for which the region is famous. But the main crop comes from the vine, which thrives in Czechoslovakia's sunniest corner; summers are hotter and drier than in western Europe.

Budapest, Hungary

Staring at each other
across the Danube are
Buda, on the left, and
Pest, on the right. The
two were not joined until
1839 when a Scotsman,
William Tierney Clark,
designed the Chain
Bridge in the middle of
the picture. In 1872 the
two towns, together with
Óbuda (old Buda), were
merged into the
Hungarian capital of
Budapest. The illuminated
Buda palace was built
in the nineteenth century.

Budapest, Hungary
(overleaf)

The settlement of Pest
grew up on the flatlands
beside the Danube,
though it was frequently
flattened by the Turks.
After the revolution of
1848, Hungarians began
to build their principal
city here to make it a
worthy European capital.
Boulevards were laid out
and grand buildings went
up, among them the neo-
Gothic Parliament House
which stretches along the
river in the front of the
picture. It was completed
in 1904.

LEO MEIER

Matthias Church, Budapest, Hungary (right)

Hungarian kings were not born royal; they had to be elected, like presidents. Matthias Corvinus was elected in 1458 and ruled for 32 years, during which time he founded a university and an observatory, encouraged the arts, built up a large library, and extended and decorated this church in Budapest. St Matthias's was the coronation church of the Hungarian kings, but in the nineteenth century it was substantially rebuilt and the coloured roof added. Inside is a treasure-house of history.

Heroes' Square, Budapest, Hungary (above)

From here even the Angel Gabriel is looked down upon. His statue tops a pillar in the middle of Budapest's Heroes' Square: at its base are Prince Árpád and six other Magyar warrior chiefs who blazed a trail through the country in AD 896, 1000 years before this monument was begun. Between the columns of the semicircular colonnade are Hungary's rulers.

LEO MEIER

THE EASTERNERS

YUGOSLAVIA BULGARIA GREECE ROMANIA TURKEY

I n the southeast of Europe one feels the breath of Asia. Although it may be said that here, in classical Greece, European civilization was born, today the countries that lie between the Adriatic and the Black seas are the least European parts of Europe. They also form the least homogenous part of the continent. Romania and Bulgaria are orthodox communist countries gradually evolving into capitalist democracies. Yugoslavia, for many years a multi-ethnic federation governed by its own brand of independent communism, is in a state of flux. Greece, where the idea of democracy was conceived, and Turkey, only a small portion of which lies within Europe at all, are democratic republics. Albania, the last hard-line Communist People's Republic in Europe, is out of step with all its neighbours, and the poorest country of the continent.

But then none of these countries is naturally rich. Romania has oilfields which have been, during the twentieth century, one of Europe's chief strategic prizes. Yugoslavia has

---

Metéora, Greece (left)

To reach the 16 monasteries at Metéora, in central Greece, monks were either hauled up in nets or boxes attached to ropes, or they ascended ladders which could be pulled up in case of attack.

Piran, Istra, Yugoslavia (previous pages)

The sun sets over the marshes and lagoons near Piran in Istra. This peninsula, which juts into the Adriatic Sea just below Trieste, has belonged to Austria, Italy and now Yugoslavia during the course of this century.

251

bauxite. Turkey has chrome. The vast majority of these peoples, however, have always lived severely, by agriculture and pastoralism in terrain that is often harshly demanding. Sometimes it is hard to realize that one is in Europe at all, so remote do these hard flinty places feel from the lush meadows and grand mountain landscapes of the west. The Turkish metropolis of Istanbul, *né* Constantinople, is indeed almost an epitome of Asianism, crowned as it is by minarets and clamouring with bazaars directly upon the Bosporus which is Asia's frontier. And on the island of Crete, the greatest of Greece's innumerable offshore islands, there are times when the sky is darkened by dust-clouds blowing across the sea from Libya.

Spiritually, too, these countries are instinct with the exotic. The legends of classical Greece speak of an ancient world which looked to the east for its sources of inspiration and delight. The glorious Byzantine buildings which ornament the region remember a time when the epicentre of Europe was on the edge of Asia. The cities are often like Levantine cities, pungent with spice and acumen. The Orthodox Christianity which prevails in these parts is a scented, mystical, hauntingly lyrical version of the creed, and the local histories are full of eastern intruders – Persians, Mongols, Russians, Turks.

Turks especially, because for several centuries almost all these territories formed part of the Ottoman Empire. The Turkish armies were turned back at the gates of Vienna in 1529, but it was not until the twentieth century that they were obliged to withdraw from the last of their European conquests. For much of their modern history, then, these countries lived under Islam – Greece itself, that lodestar of democrats everywhere, being the first to throw off the thrall and thus to kindle among the Europeans a Byronic passion for national liberty which has been intermittently blazing ever since.

Yet Islam, and the Asia that conceived it, has never quite withdrawn from these regions of Europe. In some parts it remains a living religion. There are some 80 000 practising Muslims in Bulgaria; in Yugoslavia whole towns and villages are still predominantly Muslim; and in Albania Islam was the almost universal religion until, in 1967, all religion was officially abolished. In many other regions, even in Greece itself, it remains an elusive echo, expressed in old buildings, in attitudes and values, in the way a woman wears her shawl or a man strikes a deal. Asia is present in Europe still, in these chequered countries of the continental east.

Bucharest, Romania

Rolled out like a patterned carpet for the city's dignitaries, Union Boulevard in Bucharest leads to Romania's parliament building. To create this tree-lined street of apartment blocks and new shops, many historic buildings had to come down.

LEO MEIER

Mostar, Yugoslavia (above)

The bridge at Mostar is one of the most photographed monuments in Yugoslavia. The 90-foot (27-metre) span, at the heart of the city's Turkish Old Town, was built in 1556 on the site of a Roman bridge. Young daredevils dive from the high point of the bridge into the fast-running waters below.

Sava River valley, Slovenia, Yugoslavia (right)

The crops seem well combed around this isolated church and graveyard in the Sava River valley in Slovenia. The river rises near here in the Karavanke mountains, which resemble the neighbouring Austrian Alps, and flows southeast to meet the Danube at Belgrade. The region is popular for walking and skiing.

Durmitor mountains, Yugoslavia (overleaf)

Huddled like a family of sleeping prehistoric animals, the Durmitor mountains in the heart of Monte-negro are the most dramatic in Yugoslavia. Rising to 8270 feet (2520 metres) they are the harsh homeland of a rugged people who have never been subjugated. A national park now includes rich meadows, forests and lakes, as well as mountain peaks.

Dubrovnik, Yugoslavia (above)

The beautiful walled city of the once powerful republic
of Dubrovnik is the battered star of the Dalmatian coast.
The large, white, red-roofed building just above the
port is the twelfth-century rector's palace. Fourteenth-
century convents still guard its gates.

Belgrade, Yugoslavia (overleaf)

This is the skyline of a city that has tried to keep a low profile. Belgrade, capital of Yugoslavia since 1918, has been a door to central Europe that has been so often broken down that little is left of its past. One single mosque and the Turkish fortress of Kalemegdan are about the sum of pre-nineteenth-century building.

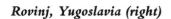

Rovinj, Yugoslavia (right)

Rovinj, on the Istran peninsula in Yugoslavia, is a town of two parts. Beneath is a grubby, grey-streaked tumble of houses. Above is the clean-lined St Euphemia, its cool campanile, modelled on St Mark's in Venice, made more striking by the deep flat blue of the Adriatic Sea. What cannot be seen from here are the twisting streets which are home to a thriving artists' colony.

259

LEO MEIER

Alexander Nevski Memorial Church, Sofia, Bulgaria (right)

Five hundred years of Turkish occupation did not extinguish Sofia's Christian faith. In 1878 Bulgaria was 'liberated' from the Turks by the Russians, and in gratitude this gold-topped church was built. The Alexander Nevski Memorial Church at the heart of the country's capital is named after a thirteenth-century prince who was patron saint of Alexander II, Tsar of Russia at the time of the liberation.

LEO MEIER

LEO MEIER

Shipka Pass, Bulgaria (above)

Above Shipka Pass, in the heart of the Balkan mountain range, is a monument to Russian soldiers and Bulgarian volunteers who died here in winter 1877–78 during the Russo–Turkish war. The pass connects the town of Gabrovo in the north with the Valley of Roses in the south.

Varna, Bulgaria (overleaf)

The tourists have landed! These half-dozen hotels north of Varna on the Black Sea seem like spaceships stopping off on a lonely planet for repairs. The inland sea, shared by Asia, is Eastern Europe's playground. It covers 164 000 square miles (425 000 square kilometres) and is fed by several rivers, notably the Danube, which makes it fairly salt free.

263

Belogradchik, Bulgaria (right)

The twisting mounds and stacks of weathered sandstone around Belogradchik can take on human or animal forms. In the extreme northwest corner of Bulgaria just below the Danube, the Roman Empire's northern boundary, they provided natural strongholds which the Romans and Turks were quick to exploit: the fort of Kaleto is at the foot of the hills in this picture. Nearby are the extensive caves of Magura, where paintings in bat guano were made in the early Bronze Age.

Rila, Bulgaria (above)

High up in the Rila mountains near the border with Greece, Ivan of Rila founded this monastery in the tenth century, and it was reconstructed some 400 years later. Today the monks' cells are guestrooms, and most of the complex is a museum. Its treasures of artworks and icons and 16000 manuscripts and books printed on the premises were accumulated beyond the gaze of the occupying Turks.

266

Athens, Greece

Democracy, philosophy, drama . . . all the essentials of western civilization crystallized around this great limestone table. At its summit is the Parthenon, built between 447 and 432 BC by Pericles and containing a large gold and ivory statue of the city's protectress, Athena. The Greek citadel and refuge was approached from the west through the Propylaia, a series of buildings which included a temple to Athena Nike. Below it is the Odeion of Herodes Atticus, an open-air theatre built in AD 161.

TIMM RAUTERT/VISUM

GUIDO ALBERTO ROSSI

Mykonos, Greece (above)

However many tourists go to the Greek island of Mykonos
every year, they cannot spoil its glaring loveliness. Nothing
can dim the dazzling white cubes of its houses standing
over the darkest of seas. There are several privately owned
Orthodox chapels, like the one in the left of the picture.

Corinth Canal, Greece (right)

Ancient Greeks wanting to sail from the Gulf of Corinth
to the Saronic Gulf would sometimes drag their boats
across the 4-mile (6-kilometre) isthmus between mainland
Greece and the Peloponnese. It wasn't until 1893 that a
canal was properly dug to shorten the trip. For sailors it is
a claustrophobic experience: the walls rise vertically on
each side, and it is barely wider than a ship's beam.

Santoríni, Greece (overleaf)

The volcanic island of
Santoríni in the southern
Cyclades is famed for its
spectacular cliff wall which
rises out of the sea. From here
the land's altitudes are not
evident. Instead there is a
pattern of fields and the
tendrils of thin roads leading
from the white flare of a town.

Gratarul, Romania

Who will make the effort
to go to Gratarul church
this Sunday to pray? It is
not in fact miles from
anywhere, but just 5 miles
(8 kilometres) outside the
small city of Călăraşi,
southeast Romania. This
region of floodplains of
the Danube just east of
Bucharest is very fertile.
There are few walls or
windbreaking trees to stop
the late-summer harvesting
machines from threshing
from one horizon to
another. Only the church
might get in the way.

GEORG GERSTER

Ploieşti, Romania

These are the shapes of twentieth-century industry: spheres and cylinders, sheds and smokestacks, pipes and drums. The Brazi petrochemical plant near the oil fields of Ploieşti north of Bucharest covers 1235 acres (500 hectares) and processes a quarter of the country's crude oil. Set up in 1934, it was greatly expanded in the 1960s. The 50 specialized units convert crude oil into more than 100 different products, including refined petrol, carbolic acid and raw material for the plastics industry.

GEORG GERSTER

GEORG GERSTER

Harman, Transylvania, Romania

This fifteenth-century church at Harman, Transylvania, needed more than prayers to protect it from the constant danger of Turkish attack. The local people built the encircling fortification, surrounded by a moat and reached by a drawbridge. Its walls are 40 feet (12 metres) high and about 13 feet (4 metres) thick.

277

The Arc de Triomphe is seen here from a balloon some 20 years after Nadar first photographed Paris from the air. Georges Eugene Haussman, who had redesigned the city, was still alive, but he had been dismissed for costing the tax-paying citizens too much money. He died in relative poverty, and this is his legacy: a radiant city of boulevards and apartment blocks familiar to millions of foreigners and French people alike.

aerial photograph (now lost). Nadar lived in an age of invention; after his first pictures other techniques were soon tried. Dry plates, shorter exposure time, hand-held cameras, roll film, all began to emerge in the next two decades, and practitioners took off from all over Europe.

Balloons were not the only way into the air. Kites were being developed, and once again it was a Frenchman, Arthur Batut, who was the photographic pioneer. In 1889 he mounted a box camera on a kite, and a rubber band on the shutter was released by a burning fuse. By sending up two camera-carrying kites he could produce a stereo effect, showing the earth's contours. Thus began the invaluable use of photography by map makers.

Rockets came next. Ludwig Rahrmann, a German, patented a missile which would explode over the vista it wanted to capture, ejecting a camera attached to a parachute. The pictures were sometimes rather crooked, but probably no more so than those snapped by pigeons, initially under another German patent taken out by Julius Neubronner in 1903. Pigeons had already proved themselves strategically important in the Franco-Prussian war, when they were used to send dispatches and micro photographs in and out of the besieged city of Paris. (During this war Nadar was made a captain and

cartoonist and photographer who called himself Nadar.

In 1868, when Emperor Napoléon III's town planner Georges Eugene Haussmann was building a new Paris with grand boulevards, Nadar photographed the city from a captive balloon 1700 feet (518 metres) above the Hippodrome. In these historic pictures, the wide, empty streets are clearly visible radiating from the recently com-

pleted Arc de Triomphe. At that time Claude Monet, age 27, was gathering impressionists around him at the Café Guerbois, a Prussian invasion was imminent, and the Eiffel Tower had not been thought of.

Ten years earlier, above the valley of the Bievre on the southern outskirts of Paris, Nadar had overcome the effects of his balloon's gas on his collodion photographic plates and taken the first recognized

281

put in charge of a balloon corps.) When the Wright brothers flew their early machines, they didn't have a hand free to take photographs. But in 1908 there was space for a passenger: a news cameraman, L.P. Bonvillain, filmed a demonstration flight over Camp d'Auvors near Le Mans in France. A decade later, during the last year of the Great War, British pilots took 6.5 million pictures.

In the Second World War the effort to maintain constant photographic reconnaissance was increased, and at its height the Mediterranean Allied Photo Reconnaissance Wing was taking 3 million pictures a month. In July 1944 this courageous, unarmed squadron lost one of its most experienced flyers, the 44-year-old French author Antoine de Saint-Exupéry, who had given a whole generation's imagination wings with his descriptions of flying in *Wind, Sand and Stars* and *Night Flight*. Serving under the same command was Beaumont Newhall, the US photography historian whose 1969 book *Airborne Camera* is still the most comprehensive on the subject.

The strategic significance of aerial photography was undeniable, and as in many fields of scientific endeavour, the military has pioneered its continued development, funding research for equipment that will take pictures further and further out in space. By 1960 detailed photographs could be taken of the earth from 50 000 feet (18 300 metres), by the US Air Force U2 'Spy Planes'. The following year a spacecraft was able to warn the world that a hurricane was on the way.

There is still a pioneering spirit among aerial photographers closer to earth. Each develops his or her own style, and many adapt equipment to their specific needs. They now have at their disposal balloons and blimps, helicopters, planes and parachutes. But however they are propelled and whatever skills and techniques they may possess, each assignment is only successful when a number of factors all come together at the right time. Some of these need determination and organization, others rest in the lap of the

ALFRED G.BUCKHAM/TOM JACOBSON

This photograph of Tower Bridge and the River Thames, titled *Gateway to London*, was taken by Captain Alfred G. Buckham around 1920. Buckham was the best-known British aerial photographer between the wars. An artist and lecturer in photographic processing, he brought his talents to the darkroom, where images were heightened, adapted and added to: he was particularly fond of imposing cloudy skies. He flew with the photographic section of the Royal Naval Air Service in the First World War, crashing nine times, the last time so severely that his larynx was removed and a breathing tube inserted in his neck. Undaunted, Buckham continued his work in cavalier spirit, capturing his best pictures in all weathers between 1000 and 2000 feet. He took his pictures standing up in the passenger seat of an open aircraft to avoid the vibrating side of the cockpit, explaining, 'If one's leg is tied to the seat with a scarf or a piece of rope, it is possible to work in perfect security'.

MICHAEL FREEMAN

MICHAEL FREEMAN

cameras aloft. All the time they remain under complete control, using remote facilities on the ground in the back of a customized Jeep and a lorry equipped with crane, winch, compressor and command centre. From there Riha has a continual bird's-eye view through a colour video monitor linked by optical fibres to a video camera on the blimp. In this way he can get to within 3 feet (1 metre) of his subject, revealing architectural detail that only pigeons have been able to appreciate before.

One of the greatest steps forward in aerial photography has been not further out into space, but nearer to the ground. Georg Riha, the

Austrian photographer (above right), has developed a 'blimp', a balloon that can carry 300 pounds (135 kilograms) of still and video

gods. A single photograph may take weeks, if not months to obtain.

Most frustratingly the photographer is completely at the mercy of the weather, which is notoriously changeable in almost all of Europe. So many opportunities can be missed, so many well-organized trips and expensive flights washed out or clouded over.

Timing is essential. Photographers in fixed-wing planes must know exactly where to get the pilot to head for and know precisely when to take the shots, because there is no going back. Pollution is a further hazard. During rush hour, visibility over a city such as London can be reduced 40 percent.

Permits, red tape and bureaucracy are daunting, and have been since a French balloonist named Triboulet had his glass plates exposed by a Customs Officer when he attempted to enter Paris in 1879. Some buildings in Europe are permanently off-limits; royalty does not like to be looked down upon. Some Cold War suspicion remains; every aerial photograph taken in Sweden must be shown to military authorities. In eastern Europe, where aerial photography has been the sole prerogative of the military, new ground has to be broken with patience.

In the end, of course, *Over Europe*'s rooftop Grand Tour of the World looks like a breeze, as if every

day were clear and every part of the continent were at peace with its neighbours and itself. We live in hope. The airborne photographers may have flown on to their next pioneering adventures, but they have left behind a trail of haunting and evocative images for us to share. Their view of Europe has permanently captured a world emerging from a century marked by war and division, from decades of dull borders guarding forbidden skies. They have shown us what the whole of Europe looks like when you let in the light.

– *Roger Williams*

Torbjörn Andersson

Born Gävle, Sweden, 1942; now living in Malmö. Andersson is one of Sweden's most distinguished photojournalists. Since 1960 he has worked for *Arbetet*, *Aftonbladet* and *Expressen*. He has won World Press Photo Awards and ten national awards, including Photographer of the Year in 1989 for his coverage of the uprising in Tiananmen Square. He has published six books.

Yann Arthus-Bertrand

Born in 1946; now living at Les Mesnuls, Paris. From 1976 Arthus-Bertrand, France's top aerial photographer, covered stories for major international magazines, including *Paris-Match*, *Figaro*, *Stern*, *Geo* and *The Sunday Times*. Since 1986 he has specialized in aerial projects, and a dozen of his thirty books are views from above, the best known of which are *Paris Seen from the Sky* and *Kenya Seen from the Sky*.

Max Dereta

Born Zagreb, Yugoslavia, 1950; now living in Almere, Holland. Dereta is one

of Europe's top skydiving photographers, though he trained as a graphic designer and has eight comic books to his credit. In 1975 he moved to Holland, and was able to combine his hobby with work. His sport, adventure and travel features have appeared in two dozen magazines, including *Cosmopolitan* and *Nieuwe Revu*. He won a World Press Photo Award in 1986 and published his first book, *Parachuting, Skydiving and Other Para Sports*, the following year.

Georg Gerster

Born Winterthur, Switzerland, 1928; now living in Zurich. Regarded as the doyen of aerial photographers, Gerster has a Ph.D. in German literature and philosophy and for six years was science editor of the Zurich weekly *Weltwoche*. As a writer-photographer, he has had assignments all over the world, from Alaska to Antarctica, from Africa to China, and he has been a regular contributor to *Neue Zurcher Zeitung*, the *National Geographic* magazine and *Geo*. He has seventeen books to his credit, three of them with Weldon Owen.

Leo Meier

Born Wolhusen, Switzerland, 1951; now living in Sydney, Australia. Meier trained as a graphic artist before emigrating to Australia in 1972. In 1981 he became chief photographer for the New South Wales National Parks and Wildlife Service, and he has been actively involved with nature conservation.

Most of his dozen books of photography have been about nature and wildlife. He has contributed to many other books, including some of those published by Weldon Owen, and his work has appeared in *National Geographic* and *Geo*. In 1976 he held the world record for long-distance boomerang throwing.

Oddbjørn Monsen

Born Ålesund, Norway, 1948; now living in Oslo. Monsen spent his nine months' military service as a photographer before starting his career on the local newspaper. Six years on *Aftenposten*, Norway's leading daily, were followed by another six for a magazine publisher. He is now co-owner of a company that publishes inflight magazines and the Worldwide Fund for Nature magazine in Norway. Travel has taken him to more than fifty countries, and his photographic work for the United Nations has been exhibited in New York.

Horst Munzig

Born Mindelheim, Germany, 1933, where he still lives. Munzig began his professional career in Ireland in 1960, when his pictures of the Croagh Patrick pilgrimage appeared in *Du*. He has been travelling the world since then, and his photographs have appeared regularly in *Du*, *Life*, *Paris-Match* and *Geo*. His work has been exhibited at the Photo-Cina in Cologne and at the Photographers' Gallery, London.

Daniel Philippe

Born Brussels, Belgium, 1952, where he still lives. Philippe has two best-selling books on France, and most of his seven books involve aerial photography. Corporate and journalistic assignments divide his time equally, and his work has appeared in many magazines, including *Figaro*, *Stern* and *Gente Viaggi*.

Georg Riha

Born Vienna, Austria, 1951, where he still lives. Riha has attracted attention with his helium balloon which has a camera platform controlled from the ground via fibre optic cable. This allows him to take detailed pictures of places where manned craft may not go. After graduating from Vienna's Academy of Film and Television, he set up his own studio specializing in advertising, industrial, architectural and aerial photography. He has published thirteen books of aerial pictures of Austria.

Guido Alberto Rossi

Born Milan, Italy, 1949, where he still lives. Rossi started out as a war photographer, covering Portuguese Guinea and Southeast Asia, but in 1973 he altered course and concentrated on travel and sport, including motor racing, sailing and horse racing. Since the mid-1980s he has specialized in aerial photography (he flies his own plane), and has produced seventeen books, including titles on Venice, Rome and Florence.

Michael St Maur Sheil

Born Oxford, England, 1946, where he now lives. An Oxford graduate, Sheil had no formal photographic training, but started freelancing for *The Times Educational Supplement*. His first major assignment was on the *Reader's Digest Illustrated Guide to Britain* in 1970. His flying experience originally came from North Sea oil rigs, and he has been associated with Black Star since 1972. His travel photography has been published in *National Geographic*, *Travel & Leisure* and the *London Daily Telegraph*.

Emil Schulthess

Born Zurich, Switzerland, 1913, where he still lives. Although trained as a graphic designer, Schulthess made his mark as art director of the Swiss monthly *Du* from 1941 to 1957. He left *Du* to go freelance and has worked widely for *Life* magazine, for whom he spent five months in Antarctica; where the Schulthess Buttress in Marie Byrd Land is named after him. A great innovator, he took the first twenty-four-hour panorama of the midnight sun in 1950 and for the last twenty years he has been building his own cameras, perfecting a technique for taking 360-degree aerial panoramas.

Thomas Stephan

Born Grotzingen, near Stuttgart, Germany, 1957; now living in Munderkingen, Wurttemberg. Stephan studied photography in Dortmund and was twenty-three when he won a European Press Junior Award. Since 1982 he has been freelance, tackling a variety of subjects including archaeology and medicine, and in 1988 he won a World Press Photo Award in the Science and Technology Series. An assignment in Bolivia gave him a taste for aerial photography, and shortly afterwards he was persuading a pilot to take him up into freezing winter skies to photograph his local frost-bound countryside.

Adam Woolfitt

Born London, England, 1938, where he now lives. A graduate of Guildford School of Art, his first job was for *Photography Magazine* for which he was involved in Cartier Bresson's premiere UK exhibition. He worked for London's *Daily Telegraph Colour Magazine* from its launch in 1964, and two years later began his association with *National Geographic*. His work has appeared in many other magazines including *Geo* and *Travel & Leisure*. He also writes on the technical aspects of photography.

ACKNOWLEDGEMENTS

The producers of *Over Europe* would like to thank the following people for their valuable assistance:

Bulgaria
Anton Chakarov
Elena Chakarov
Vintislav Ivanonv
Georgy Spasov

Czechoslovakia
Mr Brezina
Milan Hajtman
Mr Kadlec
Zdenek Kaspar
Jan Malus
Karel Nemel
Petr Penkava
Ivan Rakovic
Letecka Skola
Vlastimil Valcik
Vladimir Vartelka

Denmark
Berne Bergqvist
Flemming Nyrup

France
Heide Beurton
Salvatore Di Napoli
Helen Goossens
Patricia Goupy
Arthur Howes
Lee Huebner
Emmanuelle Laudon
Alain Lecour
Richard Morgan
Dominique Thomas
Alasdair Reynolds

Germany
Ulrich Dettki
Dieter Felter
Gert Frederking
Klaus Linke
Eduard Müller
Hans J. Preiss
Hanns Ventzke

Hungary
Kécsan Fános
Kemenéy Gábor
Bugárné Borbély Ildikó
Nemeth László
Zoltan Sárvári

Italy
Maresciallo Giuseppe
   Di Chiara

Poland
Janusz Baur
Robert Jedraszewski
Bogdan Krystin
Mr Niemczycki
Malgorzata Niezabitowska
Tomasz Tomaszewski
Andrew Wysocki
Lech Zielaskowski

Romania
Vasile Brancusi
Emilia Chivu
Dorin Ivascu

Spain
Julio Dorado Alvarez

Sweden
Ingmar Hesslefors
Heidi Johanson
Per Lindstrom
Per Utterbäck
Lassi Vuorio

Switzerland
Anita Gerster
Hans Peter Ming

United Kingdom
Brigadier R W Acworth
George Andrews
Mr Babassky
Peter Block
Rick Bonsall
Dermot Clinch
Michael Cummins
G Duda
Derek Freeman
Neyla Freeman
Anne Greensall
Susan Griggs
George Hipwell
Milan Illich

Fiona Kimber
Michael Martin
Ernestine Owen
Richard Pain
Adrian Simpson
John Turley
Linda Weaver
Marjorie L. Webb

United States
Desmond Behan
Helen Cooney
Liz Cunningham
Raymond DeMoulin
Bob Firkin
Tom Jacobson
Billie Jeanne Lebda
Ann Moscicki
Ron Puglisi
Patti Richards
Rick Smolan
Laurie Wertz
Dweezil Whiteside
Laurie Winfrey

USSR
Sergei Klockov
Mr Maximov

Yugoslavia
Milomir Brkic
S Popovic

Over Europe was originated, designed, laid out and produced entirely using Apple Macintosh IIcx computers, equipped with Supermac Trinitron monitors, PLI Infinity 40 Turbo external hard drives and Data Cart 45 megabyte removable cartridges. The more than 200 Kodak Kodachrome and Ektachrome colour images were scanned for input using the Nikon LS 3500 Film Scanner and the black and white archival pictures were scanned on the Microtek Color/Grey flatbed scanner. Layout was done using Aldus Pagemaker, with type set in Adobe Type Library's Bembo Regular, Bold and Italic. Camera-ready artwork was generated on a Linotronic 300 printer, with colour thumbnails for promotional use produced on a QMS ColorScript 100 printer.

INDEX